## Other books by James Bender

# Victory Over Fear

BY JAMES BENDER

*Coward-McCann, Inc. New York*

# FOREWORD

DEAR READER, this book is an outgrowth of my work in psychological counseling. It is a simple book, written without any pretensions of profundity. I like to believe that it is based on common sense. As such, I hope it will be helpful in the solution of many common fears, tensions, and worries.

I have borrowed materials from some of my own articles that have appeared in *The Reader's Digest, American Magazine, Living for Young Homemakers, Ladies Home Journal, Journal of Living, New York Times Magazine,* and *Your Life.* I have added case histories from my files.

I wish to express my gratitude to the many authors whose works have given me inspiration and knowledge. Some of them are mentioned in the chapters and in the bibliography.

I wish to acknowledge my gratitude: to my wife, Anne Parsons Bender, for her care and patience in preparing the manuscript and for giving me the benefit of her reactions whenever I asked for them; to F. Orlin Tremaine for his "French soldier's philosophy" in Chapter 15; to the numerous friends and clients whose willingness to share their rich experience has provided many of the illustrations and examples.

James F. Bender

The National Institute for Human Relations
New York 17, N. Y.
September, 1952

# CONTENTS

# Victory Over Fear

# 1.   Join the Cult of Common Sense

A BEAUTIFUL BLONDE, twenty-eight and enormously talented—an actress in a Broadway musical—almost died from an overdose of sleeping pills. She had piled up a large debt and didn't know how to pay it off. And so, her solution was to end it all. If her brother hadn't forced his way into her apartment, a suicide would have left a lot of good-hearted creditors holding the bag.

It didn't take the psychologist very long to find out that the beautiful blonde had never lived within her income. A budget never occurred to her as a way out of her fear. She didn't think it was smart to be thrifty. She borrowed where she could; rarely met her obligations; often pawned her fur coat and jewelry. Whenever she had a good role, she spent all she made—never laid away anything for the idle days around the corner.

She got deeper and deeper in debt. The crisis came shortly after she saw on the call-board: THIS IS TO SERVE NOTICE THE LAST PERFORMANCE OF THE CURRENT RUN WILL BE ON JULY 10. The off-season was at hand; no money; no credit; insistent bill collectors. Although an excellent actress, she had no common sense in handling money. Alas, what a lot of company she has!

"Common sense," said William James, "is not sense common to everyone; but sense in common things." The famed psychologist's nice definition makes *common sense* a misnomer, doesn't it? For it appears to be rare. Many gifted men and women, mind you, are strangers to common sense in the management of their private lives. Often they have tight little compartments in their heads that keep out sensible decisions. They may write best-sellers, paint famous canvases, run successful businesses, build up thriving practices—and yet fall down when it comes to being happy, well-adjusted people.

I know a top-rung salesman who never used common sense in marrying. (He's just been divorced from his third wife.)

Gertrude —— presides over a lucrative interior decorating salon. Yet she hasn't applied common sense in educating her children.

Mabel —— is a beautiful model, but stays up all hours doing the night clubs six or seven nights a week.

A carpenter friend of mine works hard, lives frugally, and throws away his family's security on the ponies.

Nice people—all of them—but they have holes in their dikes. A little common sense would plug them up and prevent the deluge that otherwise must surely overcome them.

When you study the lives of these men and women—you have friends and neighbors in the same boat, undoubtedly—you wonder at their foolishness. It brings them so much unhappiness. And those that love them often suffer more. Usually fear plays a stellar role in the lives of those who will not be guided by common sense.

Do you remember the story of the little chick that ran wildly around the barnyard chirping that the sky was falling down? (A leaf, you will recall, had fallen on its tail.) Because the chick only recently came out of its shell, we can't be too harsh on him. But all the other animals (except one) accepted the bad news without question. They cackled, crowed, grunted, mooed, all of them contributing to the awful din, each in his own decibelic way, because they didn't stop to think.

And do you remember Orson Welles' famous radio program, back in the 'thirties, *Invasion From Mars?* Hysterical people, all over the country, actually believed the Martians were upon us and ran to the hills with all sorts of useless possessions in tow. Like the beautiful blonde actress, the chick and barnyard denizens, fear drove them to do silly things. Suppose they had put their common sense to work. What a lot of fuss and feathers they could have saved!

As I write this, the Korean crisis is in the news. People are scared. They are hoarding. They fear they will not be provided for. Take sugar, as an example. Up in the Bronx, a grocer put a sign in his window: 5 LBS. OF SUGAR 95 CENTS. His store was mobbed. Across the street, you could get five pounds of sugar at the regular price—37 cents. The papers carry pictures of huge supplies of sugar being unloaded at the docks, and reassurances from officials that there is plenty of sugar. All this information was broadcast, yet the frightened geese wouldn't use their common sense.

Hypochondriacs lack common sense as regards health. Like so many other neurotics, they allow their imagination to plunge them into despair. They seem to abhor the facts about their physical condition. If they would use their common sense, how much happier they would be to live with! The bright spot, of course, is that these fearful ones can learn to use their common sense. Once they do, their foolish fears are gone with the wind.

Usually they need someone whose judgment they respect, someone they like, to give them a push in the right direction. I can think of no better-qualified individual to do this than a *persuasive* family doctor or a clergyman. (Isn't it strange that none of the 68 medical schools in this country that are approved by the American Medical Association, teaches the art of persuasion?) The persuasive doctor "sells" his patient on helping himself to get well. He reassures. He quiets doubts. He explains his prescriptions. He appeals to common sense.

Such a one was Dr. Paul Dubois of France, particularly famous for his success with hypochondriacs. Listen to him talk common sense to one of his patients afflicted with a constipation phobia:

"You do not have to concern yourself about it (constipation). Under the influence of overfeeding and of observing a fixed hour, you may have a movement spontaneously, so that everything will be all right; or you may not have to succeed, for we have an enema to fall back upon which will always work. In all ways free yourself from anxiety. Do not let us talk any more about this symptom! You shall only tell me when you have regular movements. . . ." From that day the phobia of constipation ceased.

From time to time he would encourage her anew with "Let your mind dwell on these few simple and clear ideas: First, my whole trouble is nervous—that is to say, psychic; and as there is no lesion, my condition is curable. Second, one can always place one's pains on a lower rung of the ladder of evils and can at least manage voluntarily to forget them." Isn't this excellent common sense? What a fortunate hypochondriac to have such an excellent physician!

To me the truly most glorious aspect of human nature is that it is subject to growth at all ages. If this were not true, civilization would have had to shut up shop long ago. But the trouble is that so many of our influential healers do not preach, insinuate, and suggest the idea of health often enough to their patients.

The deepest tragedy in the lives of all of us, if I may venture the opinion, is that we are not always receptive to the truth when it confronts us. A boy of twenty makes a quickie marriage against all the wise advice given him to the contrary. A year later his wife gives birth to a girl baby. But this boy and his wife no longer love each other. They fight, separate, embitter their lives forever after. Worse, they ruin their daughter's future. If they had only used their common sense in planning ahead for a good marriage.

A man loses a position as editor of a book-publishing firm. He won't accept another position for less money or prestige. He is not humble in spirit. He spends his life on past glories. He lets his wife support him. As an embittered old man, he realizes what he should have done.

"What might have been, if I had only . . ." is perhaps the most doleful refrain of our lives. Yet it need not echo down the corridors of our future as often as it does. If every fearful person would accept this truth—We can develop common sense, we can develop insight and solve our daily problems well—he would experience a great uptake in happiness. For we *can* develop common sense, if we *want to*. Thousands upon thousands, beset with foolish fears, have found and are finding serenity and purpose in their lives, simply by joining the cult of common sense.

Yes, sense in common things is devoutly to be wished. As I write this, I have on my desk a copy of the *New York World-Telegram and Sun*. There is a photograph of a pretty woman. Above it, the headline: FLEES FROM FEAR. The story says "Mrs. —— is being sought by police of 14 states. They want to tell her she doesn't have cancer. The 30-year-old mother kissed her three young children Friday and vanished in the mistaken belief that she was suffering from cancer. Her husband learned yesterday that there was nothing seriously wrong with her." Although we can sympathize with her, we can't credit her with common sense. Flight didn't solve her problem, since fear always runs as fast as she can. Common sense would have told her: Hold on, I must face the facts. If I should have cancer, I will try to find a cure. If I don't have it, so much the better.

The other day a young wife came in to tell her story of unhappiness. She was married for six months, when she left her husband. This was a year and a half ago. Now she wants to go back to him.

"Why?"

"Well, I want the protection of a home and a husband, even if I don't love him."

"What have you got against him?" And then she rattled off this list:

"He doesn't talk to me enough." (Did he talk much before your marriage?—No, he hadn't; he was the quiet type.)

"He wants to go out with the fellows one night a week, and I don't think he should." (Won't he extend the privilege of your going out with your girl friends? Yes, I suppose so.)

"He doesn't help me with the housework." (Are four rooms too much to take care of when your husband works all day to support you?)

"He thinks too much about his mother." (Isn't there enough love for both of you? He loves his mother in a different way, you know.)

"He's unambitious." (Have you tried inspiring him to greater efforts rather than nag him?)

"He spends his pocket money foolishly." (*Pocket money* means to be spent as we please, doesn't it? Does he give you pocket money? Yes, he does.)

"He should sense when I want sexual relations and not

think of his own desires all the time." (Have you talked it over in a tender, diplomatic way? No, she hadn't.)

Obviously the young woman was as selfish as an infant. She didn't know the first principle of love: Love grows from giving; it shrinks from taking. Common sense says, How can you expect your marriage to succeed if you hold grudges? How can you make it last on the basis of only your convenience?

A young bride tries her hand at baking biscuits. First time they come out of the oven too hard, too brown. If her husband is a dolt, he will criticize them, perhaps contrast them with his mother's biscuits. And his wife will hate baking biscuits ever after. If he has some common sense, he will praise the biscuits; will eat two or three of them with gusto; will soften them up with gravy or lots of butter if he must. How grateful she will be! How she will improve the next batch!

A bridegroom comes home with a five-dollar raise; he had expected more. The foolish wife will deprecate it. "What good is five dollars these days?" she says. "Mary Smith's husband brought home a fifteen-dollar raise." The wise bride, on the other hand, will make much ado about the five-dollar raise. Which way will give the young man the urge to try harder? The technique, you see, is really very simple.

A man has been ill. Although he is recovering, he will not admit it. He continues to say he feels "terrible," "no improvement," "I'm afraid I'll always be an invalid," etc.

Then his doctor points out, "You *are* better. You are just about completely recovered. Let's face the facts. Not long ago you were down with a fever. Today your temperature is normal. Last month your urine was dark green and had a lot of ugly sediment in it. Today it's a normal amber-color and free of sediment. Your heartbeat was up to 90. Now it's back to 70. You were sallow. Now look at yourself. There is a fresh color to your skin. You know all these things as well as I do.

Why, for heaven's sake, do you go around saying you feel terrible? Why do you insist there's no improvement? Come, now, tell me the truth, don't you feel sorry for yourself? How do you really feel?"

"Why, Doctor, since you mention it, I really do feel all right again. I'm sorry I said that. I guess I must have sold myself a bill of goods—of poor health." Common sense. Yes, dear fool, you had to be lead by the nose to face the facts. You actually paid good money to discover what your common sense could have told you for nothing. Come, come! Use your head.

"Is there a simple way to develop common sense? Yes, there is. It is what you may call the questioning technique. Ask yourself—and others—questions. For example: John —— had a serious problem to solve. His wife needed an unusual surgical operation. Only a few specialists could perform that operation. Their family physician recommended Dr. X. But his fee was $1,500. Now John and his wife were in modest circumstances. They couldn't afford the fee. But notice how John's common sense came to the rescue:

"Isn't there someone else, more reasonable?"

"Yes," said the family doctor, "there's Dr. Y—a good deal younger. While he doesn't have the other man's reputation, he's certainly up and coming."

"Do you know what his fee would be?"

"No, I don't know what he'd charge you, but I'd guess—off the record—five or six hundred dollars."

"Is he recognized by the specialists in his own field?"

"Yes, he's recently been elected to the American College of Surgeons as a Fellow and also to the American Board of Surgery."

"Is his mortality rate as low as Dr. X's?"

"I can't answer that because I don't know."

"Could you introduce me to someone who has had Dr. Y?"

By pursuing questions like these, John —— and his wife decided on Dr. Y. The operation was successful, and the surgeon's fee was $500.00.

A New Jersey white-collar worker, a father of two children, asked his wife, "Honey, how can we meet the high cost of living?" She suggested that they cut down on food, eat a cheaper diet. But this didn't satisfy him. He went to the library and read up on mass purchasing.

*Buy fruits and vegetables in season and deep freeze them. Buy your meats in quantity lots. You will find periods when pork is low in price while beef is high; and vice versa. Chickens are ordinarily cheaper in summer than winter,* etc. To make a long story short, he sold his camera, and bought a deep-freeze unit. Result: stupendous savings on the food bill and a balanced budget. "And we eat better than ever." His question led to a very sound decision.

If you are a fearful person, you are probably dissatisfied with many of your decisions. Too many of them come croppers. You begin to distrust your judgment. You may even run to the astrologer to let him take the responsibility off your shoulders. You become superstitious and imagine that luck is against you. Self-doubt and fears increase.

But be not downcast. Common sense will come to your rescue, if you will only try.

Here is another way to develop common sense. Develop the art of making sound decisions. In the classes I hold for executives, I ask them how they account for the excellence of their decisions in business. They attribute it—not to any special gift—simply to common sense. And interestingly enough, they admit that the art of making sound decisions comes with trial and error; with trial and success. They do the best they can, and let the chips fall where they may. They can't afford to ruin their health or spread the contagion of fear, worry, and indecisiveness among their workers. Their recommendations are worth study.

## HOW TO MASTER THE ART OF MAKING SOUND DECISIONS

1. *Get the facts first.* We often carry away from the movies a stereotyped picture of the big business executive. On the screen, he speaks in rapid-fire order without a pause for facts. In real life, the high-powered executives don't rely on hunches. They can't afford to risk huge investments on snap judgments. Quite the contrary.

E. A. Filene in his book, *The New Leadership in Business,* says that the men who head up our large concerns, today more than ever, base their decisions on facts. They make use of experts, laboratories, market surveys, statistics, trade associations and governmental agencies.

Now, this is sound advice for us to apply to our personal problems and fears. "What are the facts?" should be uppermost in our minds. Of course we can get the facts, if we want them; if we are willing to invest some time and effort. One good friend in this respect is the public library. Here we can get facts on almost any subject. If we don't know where to look, the librarian will help.

A member of the New York Stock Exchange told me that you don't have to be a specialist to make excellent investments. He recounted how many men and women of moderate means have increased their wealth by making judicious investments. He pointed out how they study the ratings of stocks and bonds in the public library. How they look up government reports; estimates of economists; experts' opinions of short- and long-term prospects for this industry or that. They put the facts through the sieve of their common sense.

"The trouble with so many investors is," my friend said,

shaking his scolding finger at me as if I were the culprit, "they take tips and half-baked advice without checking up on them; they won't dig out facts and ask questions!"

He went on: "Too often the man in the street won't buy good securities until everyone is buying them—when they're way on top—overpriced. And you can't get him to buy stocks when they are down and cheap. He seems to lack courage, just when he should have it. The truth of the matter is, he lets fear put him through the wringer. He's afraid he'll be left out in the cold when stocks are high; and so he buys them then. He's afraid the country is going to the dogs when stocks are down, and won't touch them. He won't face facts!"

**2.** *Time your decisions right.* Make quick decisions when quick decisions are absolutely necessary. Equally important, make important decisions as carefully as possible. These ordinarily take a longer time to make.

If Joe Smith loses his job, he must decide to look for another right away. His family must eat. But what about John White who feels stymied in his present job? He can't afford to quit because he also has responsibilities. He can either let the job gnaw at his vitals, or lay solid plans for a better one. Let's assume he decides to do the latter. Then he determines the kind of job he would like; what kind he is best fitted to succeed at. He may write to his city or state Department of Education to see where he may take aptitude tests to help him decide on the basis of facts. After he discovers what fields would challenge his abilities best, he reads books and pamphlets recommended by an expert—to find out what the relative merits these fields hold. Which has the best future? Once he has clearly and realistically in mind the ideal job for him, then he lays plans for getting that job. In the meantime he holds on to the one he has. Common sense.

Five years ago a young college instructor, whom I know, decided that his growing family needed a larger income than he could earn as a teacher. He answered an advertisement in one of the New York Sunday papers. It was a training assistant's job in an airplane manufacturing company. He got it.

Six months later he answered another ad. He was now ready for more responsibility in the same field. He got that job too, at a $1,500 annual increase. Then thirteen months later, he used the same procedure to land his present position as personnel director of a fire insurance company. He began that position at $10,000.00. In two years, his well-laid plans and hardheaded decisions netted him an increase in income of almost 300 per cent! He had timed his decisions right.

Aside from his excellent native ability, he laid plans, one logical step at a time. He is too busy to be afraid. He agrees with General MacArthur: "There is no such thing as security. There is only opportunity." Did you know that approximately 84 per cent of the population are estimated to use only about 30 per cent of their abilities? And here is another fact worth remembering: The 16 per cent who use their common sense to the full have the fewest fears.

3. *Don't put if off.* Wasn't it Benjamin Franklin who called procrastination a thief? It robs a man of opportunities. For if you permit a fear to go unresolved, it grows. Edward —— sought advice about his fear to confide in his wife. During the summer, while his wife and youngster were at the seashore, he met a former sweetheart quite by accident. They had dinner together. As they were leaving the restaurant he saw his wife's best friend. Although his date with his former sweetheart was innocent enough, he feared that his wife might not believe him. He was sure that she would find out. He spent two or three sleepless nights putting off the decision to do something about it. Once he told her, his heart was light. His wife understood and said little about it. Do you remember the old Pillsbury motto: *Eventually, why not now?* It's a good one to apply to solving your fears.

Years ago I had an interesting experience that jolted me out of my tendency to procrastinate. I had an idea for an article for a magazine. But I put off writing the editor to see whether he would be interested to have the idea developed. Six months later I saw the same idea in an article, announced on the cover of the magazine I had in mind. The procrastinator doesn't win races.

A deferred decision is sometimes worse than no decision at all. It may involve more heartbreak. If you feel that you have the habit of procrastination, break it. Begin now. Make yourself do little things on time. You look at your fingernails. They need manicuring. But you say to yourself, "Oh, I'll let them go another day!" No, don't. Get after them, now. Tonight.

You want to copy an excerpt from an article you've just read. But the pencil is in the desk across the room. Your easy chair feels too comfortable, and you say, "I'll copy it later on." No. Make yourself copy it now. For by training yourself to do the little things on time, you will find the bigger, more important decisions easier to carry out promptly. "No matter how full a reservoir of *maxims* one may possess, and no matter how good one's sentiments may be," writes William James, "if one has not taken advantage of every concrete opportunity to *act,* one's character may remain entirely unaffected for the better. *With mere good intentions, hell is proverbially paved.*"

4. *Get reactions.* If you have the knack of making sound decisions you respect the judgment of others. To be sure, you don't always follow it. But you find that the thoughts of others sharpen your own critical powers. You believe that two or more heads are better than one to test the value of an opinion or decision. And so you try out your ideas on friends and associates to see how they react to them. An editor I know has dummies drawn of ideas for magazine covers.

Then he passes them out to his maid and butler and a few friends. He's particularly interested in the reactions of his servants. When they exclaim their preference, he makes a careful note of it. He watches their facial expression when they first glance at the covers. He believes that he himself is too close to the woods to see the trees and needs reader reactions. His plan pays off.

A national research organization recently made an interesting discovery: more executives write inquiries to authors of business articles six months after publication than at any time. At first blush, you may think they procrastinate. But that isn't the reason for their delay. The study also found out that the commonest reason for the time-lag is that executives talk over the article with associates—how the author's ideas or service might be used to the firm's advantage. At odd moments—as our model executive drives to work or goes on a business trip—he weighs the pros and cons of the reactions he has gathered. Once he makes the decision, he knows it is as good as he can reasonably make it. At that time he sends off the inquiry.

5. *Listen to inner promptings.* An oculist read an article describing a method of annealing two different kinds of glass into one unit. Why couldn't this idea be adapted to bifocal lenses? Why couldn't you then make spectacles without the usual dividing line that blurs the vision? He felt so strongly that he had hit on a worthy idea, he could hardly eat or sleep until he put it in effect. He sold his store. He enlisted wealthy men to get financial backing. His wife thought him foolish to give up the security of the store for a pot of gold at the other end of the rainbow. But he knew deep within him that he could do nothing else. His whole being told him that he was taking the right step. The future proved him right, for his decision paid off handsomely.

His inner prompting was of course nourished by long years

of experience with complaints about bifocals. He had discovered the solution to a very old problem in his field. He knew himself well enough to realize that he was not given to swallowing half-baked ideas. Finally, he could do nothing else then cast his lot with the new idea. It was stronger than any opposing argument.

Leaders in many fields nourish the inner prompting; they listen to it. Yet they don't go off half-cocked. They make use of their experience and past judgments. They weigh the inner prompting carefully. They weigh it by getting all the facts, by timing their decisions right, by avoiding procrastination, by getting the reactions of others. These are the steps you and I can also take to develop the art of making sound, yes *sounder,* decisions. And we shall grow in confidence. And the fear of beginning, of doing, of deciding—will be ours no more.

## 2.  Study the Anatomy of Fear

IF YOU ARE LOOKING for a motto to wear on your shield, may I suggest *sapere aude*—"Dare to know!" Surely these are brave words for warriors against fear to live by. For fear, like ignorance, abhors facts. When we know how fear affects body, mind, and temperament, we have a double-edged sword for our fight on fear.

One edge of the sword we call *sublimation*. It represents the way we can turn our knowledge of fear into great, positive effort. As we shall see, fear can make us stronger physically, more alert than we ordinarily are.

The other edge of the sword we name *prevention*. Once we know fear's symptoms, we can actually sidestep many of them. And that is an excellent way—the least troublesome way—to deal with fear.

Let us begin our survey of facts about fear with definitions. *Fear,* according to Webster, is "painful emotion caused by alarm." Fear is a general term. It covers fright, dismay, consternation, panic, terror and horror.

*Fright* implies the shock of sudden, startling, short-lived fear. You are in your armchair, reading a book. Everything is quiet—when all of a sudden you hear an explosion. You jump out of your skin. (Psychologists call this the *startle reflex*. Everybody's got it except idiots and those suffering from certain diseases, such as epilepsy.) Then someone tells you an excavator in the next block is blasting rock, and your fright quickly goes away.

*Dismay* means to deprive of spirit, initiative, or courage by an alarming prospect. A salesman is dismayed by the news of his sales manager's death. He wonders whether his job will be secure under the new sales manager.

*Consternation* implies a virtual paralysis of the faculties as the result of fear. You see a boa constrictor slithering down a tree in front of you, and your resulting fear transfixes you so that you can't move.

*Panic* is an overmastering fear that seizes groups, much like cattle in a stampede. You are enjoying a movie. Suddenly somebody yells "Fire!" You join the mob in its mad rush. Later on, you learn it was a false alarm, and you feel rather sheepish for running without using your head.

*Terror* suggests violent fright, as when you have a nightmare.

*Horror* has the implicaton of shuddering, such as you might experience if you were to see a man, unaware of his danger, murdered.

All these synonyms identify various degrees of a state of body and mind we call fear. Someone has said that we think of fear as nothing more or less than anticipated pain. The most important thing to remember about all *these* fearful states is that they are conscious; we are ordinarily aware of the immediate cause of such fears. And our immediate reaction to them is the desire to run away from them.

On the other hand, the cause of *Anxiety* is not so obvious. Anxiety is a painful uneasiness of mind over something in the future, something unknown, something we often can't flee from. It is vague; not definite. You can't put your finger on the precise cause of it. Or, you may lay it to a number of ill-defined apprehensions. "I can't tell you just why I feel so uneasy," a forty-five year-old woman said to me the other day. "I have no money worries, and my health is pretty good. But I have strange forebodings that keep me jittery." She gave an excellent definition of anxiety because she couldn't give a cause for it.

*Phobia* is also irrational. Unlike anxiety, it is a persistent dread of a particular object or situation. Psychologists consider the phobia as neurotic symptoms. In the typical case of simple phobia, the individual seems normal, except that he shrinks in dread from some particular object, such as a dog; or situation, such as being in a closed room. If, by accident, he meets a dog or finds himself in a closed room, he suffers intense and uncontrollable dread. And reassurance or appeal to his reason doesn't help him overcome his phobia. (In Appendix A you will find a list of the common phobias.)

An eighteen-year-old stutterer reported for his appointment quite out of breath. Since my office is on the ninth floor, I suspected he had climbed the stairs. "I like to climb stairs," he said, "because I develop my breath capacity that way." Then we discovered he was ashamed to admit his phobia of riding in an elevator. This is the story:

When he was three years old, his uncle took him for a ride on a freight elevator where he worked. A cat was asleep in a corner of the elevator. As the boy ran around, he accidentally tramped on the cat. It clawed him and set up a loud screech. The boy became hysterical. The uncle didn't tell the boy's parents about it.

Curiously enough, the boy has no phobia of cats, although he doesn't like them. His phobia attached itself to elevators. One fact in this case is typical of the phobias: the boy didn't remember its onset until, as a result of interpretation of his dreams and word-associations, the details were pieced together. After that his phobia gradually disappeared.

Anxiety is present in every neurosis and in almost every mental disease. Phobias may be present. Anxiety and phobias are deeply distressing states. We know from those who have suffered from mental disturbance, such as depression, schizophrenia, compulsions, that no physical suffering can compare with anxiety and phobia. We can get release from physical pain rather easily. But anxiety can last so long and relief from it can be exceedingly difficult to get. As Shakespeare said, "Present fears are less than horrible imaginings."

Anxiety and phobias, as defined here, are not ordinarily solved without expert help. To the man or woman suffering from deep anxiety or a troublesome phobia the best advice is, enlist the aid of a qualified psychologist or psychiatrist. Make sure that the specialist is a member of either the American Psychological Association or the American Psychiatric Association.

In other words, you yourself can triumph over the common fears of everyday life. But anyone runs a grave risk if he tries to find the answer to his phobias and anxiety states without expert help. The advice we often hear—"Do the thing you fear"—may be good advice so long as applied to fear. If applied to anxiety or phobias, it may be downright dangerous.

For example, if you are afraid of speaking before an audience because you have never had the experience of doing so, you can probably get over it by taking a public-speaking course. You then conquer your fear by doing the thing you fear. But suppose your phobia were jumping off high buildings . . . ?

That's why the intelligent man or woman studies to understand fear. "Fear springs from ignorance," says Emerson. Certainly, our control of fear grows stronger and surer as we develop our understanding of its strange and marvelous ways.

Fear, like any other base emotion, transforms body, mind and attitude. The changes are powerful and often quite full of harm to health and peace of mind, unless we control them.

To appreciate how fear changes the body processes we must remember the pair of powerful, ductless glands, the *suprarenals*. These dynamos are situated right above the kidneys. Whenever we fear or get angry or feel pain, the suprarenals discharge adrenin, more commonly called adrenalin, into the blood stream. So soon as the heart circulates the blood, so quickly does adrenalin take effect. Among other things it stimulates the liver to release sugar into the blood—sugar, the source of muscular energy.

That explains why the individual under the influence of a powerful emotion is actually stronger than at other times. Under the impetus of fear, people do really superhuman feats. I once knew a slight, middle-aged bookkeeper to lift an overturned Model T Ford high enough for his wife to crawl out from under it. The fear for her life, following a Sunday-afternoon accident, gave him the strength he had never had before.

Or, take the amazing exploit of John Colter as another instance. Some Montana Indians seized Colter and a friend in 1880. The friend resisted them, and they tortured him to death. Then they stripped Colter naked and signaled him to run. He understood that he was to run a race for his life. He started like a deer, and each time he heard warwhoops behind him he increased his speed. After running for three miles his strength began to ebb. As he looked back, only one Indian was close on to him. The Indian rushed forward and threw the spear at Colter. Colter seized the spear, killed the Indian, and ran "with renewed strength, feeling as if he had not run a mile."

Fear had helped him to run faster than he knew he was capable of running. It was fear also that gave him his "second wind." Psychologists believe that nature developed these immense reservoirs of strength to preserve our lives. Ages ago, when a saber-toothed tiger approached, our fear of it provided us with enormous energy to escape. And as we fled, our muscles burned up sugar, the source of energy, released from the liver by the secretions of the suprarenals.

But here's the rub: today the suprarenals react to fear in the same way as in the days of the saber-toothed tiger. Instead of using up the energy in great muscular activity, we sit at our desks or in our armchairs. Result is, the sugar continues to float in the blood stream until the kidneys gradually work it off. If too much adrenalin is secreted too often by recurrent emotional upsets, *glycosuria* develops. This is the condition of sugar in the blood. Chronic glycosuria sometimes leads to diabetes. In other words, physicians have discovered that some people develop diabetes because they are too fearful or too frequently angry. The great Charles Darwin in his *Origin of the Emotions* lists many of the physical symptoms of great fear.

Fear is often preceded by astonishment, and is so far akin to it that both lead to the senses of sight and hearing being instantly aroused. In both cases the eyes and the mouth are widely opened and the eyebrows raised. The frightened man at first stands like a statue, motionless and breathless, or crouches down as if instinctively to escape observation. The heart beats quickly and violently so that it palpitates or knocks against the ribs; but it is very doubtful if it then works more efficiently than usual, so as to send a greater supply of blood to all parts of the body; for the skin instantly becomes pale as during incipient faintness. This paleness of the surface, however, is probably in large part, or is exclusively, due to the vaso-motor centre being affected in such a manner as to cause the contraction of the small arteries of the skin. That the skin is much affected under the sense of great fear, we see in the marvellous manner in which perspiration immediately exudes from it. This exudation is all the more remarkable, as the surface is then cold, and hence the term, a cold sweat; whereas the sudorific (sweat) glands are properly excited into action when the surface is heated. The hairs also on the skin stand erect, and the superficial muscles shiver. In connection with the disturbed action of the heart the breathing is hurried. The salivary glands act imperfectly; the mouth becomes dry and is often opened and shut. I have also noticed that under slight fear there is stronger tendency to yawn. One of the best marked symptoms is the trembling of all the muscles of the body; and this is often first seen in the lips. From this cause, and from the dryness of the mouth, the voice becomes husky or indistinct or may altogether fail. As fear increases into an agony of terror, we behold as under all violent emotions, diversified results. The heart beats wildly or must fail to act and faintness ensue; there is a death-like pallor; the breathing is labored; the wings of the nostrils are widely dilated; there is a gasping and convulsive motion of the lips, a tremor on the hollow cheek, a gulping and catching of the throat; the uncovered and protruding eyeballs are fixed on the object of terror; or they may roll restlessly from side to side. The pupils are said to be enormously dilated. All the muscles of the body may become rigid or may be thrown into convulsive movements. The hands are alternately clenched and opened, often with a twitching movement. The arms may be protruded as if to avert some dreadful danger, or may be thrown wildly over the head. The Rev. Mr. Hageauer has seen this latter action in a terrified Australian. In other cases there is a sudden and uncontrollable tendency to headlong flight; and so strong is this that the boldest may be seized with a sudden panic. These symptoms describe fear of the extreme sort.

Are there any other physical symptoms? Yes, many that we can't see. For example, Dr. Ferrari examined samples of blood from students before and after they took examinations. In students just after an examination he found an average of 457,000 more red corpuscles per cubic millimeter than in the same students before the examination—the higher corresponding to the excited, the lowest to an "indifferent and phlegmatic" member of the group.

Physiologists and psychologists have discovered other physical symptoms of fear. Many of these symptoms we can't observe outside the laboratory. Yet they play their part in preparing the body for emergencies.

For example:

1. Fear alters the distribution of blood in the body, driving it from the organs in the abdominal cavity into the heart, lungs, limbs, and central nervous system.
2. Adrenalin emptied into the blood stream as the result of fear makes the coagulation of the blood more rapid.
   Again, one of nature's preservatives of life in a crisis. If the wounded fighter's blood did not coagulate, he would bleed to death.
3. Fear increases muscular efficiency.
4. Fear restores energy to fatigued muscles.
5. Fear increases breathing and reduces carbon dioxide in the blood.

Fear changes the body in many other ways—ways that were particularly useful in less civilized times. Our big problem today is to control the symptoms of fear so that they do not make us ill. For our civilization discourages us from "working off" the body symptoms by fighting or running. Tom Smith, the financier, who loses his shirt in Wall Street, may have as a result many of the symptoms that John Colter had when the Indians stripped him. But Smith can't very well escape running cross-country as Colter did. Unlike Colter, Smith's excessive adrenalin is actually a physical handicap to him in his office. For the fact seems to be that the symptoms of fear are outmoded for the times we live in. In other words, our physical symptoms of fear are obsolete. Our only hope is to learn to control them through understanding.

Up to now we have reviewed together the physical symptoms of fear. How, then, does fear affect thinking? In the first place fear tends to make us more resourceful. A spy, waiting to be shot, because of his fear of death will devise ways of escape that would not occur to him in the comfort and security of his home.

The fear of being trampled by a stampeding herd will speed up our analysis of the landscape—will make us see the tree quicker and help us reach it and climb it faster.

In other words, when we are propelled into a crisis that makes us fearful, we can rely on our thinking processes to click fast. This is all to the good.

When, however, we *imagine* ourselves in fearful crises we use our thoughts to make us unhappy. We may in this way fear unemployment when the prospects are virtually nonexistent. We may fear that our parents will die of a malignant disease although they are robust. We may fear the loss of friendships when we have always been loyal and cordial to our friends. Such chronic fears keep us on continual edge. They destroy our sense of well-being. They make serious inroads on our efficiency and health. They are therefore said to be symptoms of an *anxiety neurosis*.

The fact that the "worrier" anticipates unhappiness when

it is improbable is significant. Some unhappy experience in the "worrier's" early life predisposes him to anxiety. Of course all of us at times experience imagined fears or anxieties. But most of us throw them off in the course of meeting our daily responsibilities.

Some of us by temperament seem to entertain imaginary fears more frequently than others because of the nature of our so-called mood cycles. As you know, psychologists have demonstrated that periodically all of us feel somewhat depressed. During these times, imagined fears people our thoughts, unless we take preventive steps. These depressive periods recur about every four weeks. Ordinarily they don't last long, being followed immediately by moods of well-being and elation. Some of us have much different mood swings or cycles than others. All of us have them.

Your mood cycle probably resembles one of the three "normal" or common types:

*Type A, the elated:* If your mood cycle is of this type, you are optimistic, and elated for longer periods than you are depressed. Moreover, your depression doesn't get very deep. That means that your imagined fears of anxieties are neither as numerous nor as serious as type B.

*Type B, the depressed:* This type is the reverse of type A. In type A we see that the periods of depression that come, remain longer than the periods of elation. If your mood cycle approximates type B, you are likely to have more imagined fears and you tend to linger over them longer than those whose mood cycles are type A.

*Type C, the matured:* Type C is the one that brings the most happiness and satisfaction. For here are no great deviations from the level keel. Those whose mood cycles conform pretty much to the type C pattern have the fewest imagined fears. They keep their moods well in hand. They are said to be emotionally mature. Before we consider ways and means to control our mood cycles, let us understand them better.

As a student of human nature, you realize that some people are more even of temperament than others. Some are so unpredictable—they swing from violent elation to profound depression—that they have to be hospitalized. Others evidently are always calm or happy. Still others seem to be happy much of the time with only an occasional lapse into gloom.

If you were to study any one of these people at close range and intensively for a month or longer, you would have evidence that they vary from day to day in their moods. The variations may be slight and their symptoms hidden from casual acquaintances. But you would observe them steadily from your close vantage point.

Dr. Rexford B. Hersey, of the University of Pennsylvania, studied many workers on the job for longer than a year. He discovered that all of them had characteristic up and down swings of moods; that the majority of them went from low to high, back to low again—in other words, made a complete cycle—once every twenty-eight days. However, some of them experienced only one complete cycle every ninety days; others completed more than nine cycles in the same number of days!

We can make use of the conclusions drawn by Dr. Hersey and other psychologists. We can relate them to our exploration of fear:

1. When your mood cycle is at low point, when you feel that life is bleak and imagined fears come crowding in, you will begin to enter the upward phase.
2. When your viewpoint is marked by elation, freedom from

fear, and optimism—when you wonder how you ever be-come blue and discouraged—this is the time when the downswing is about to begin.

3. At the crest of your mood cycle, you take bad news in your stride. Whatever fears you feel have a minimum impact on you at that time. You see a solution to them. Your phys-ical energy, appetite, and sleep all are at their best. You see great possibilities in your plans. Your future looks bright.

4. When you sink into the trough of your cycle, the reverse is true. Then even good news lacks luster. You tend to be pessimistic. Your energy is low; food and sleep aren't as rewarding as they were at the crest. Life generally seems full of obstacles. You may even think that plans for your future are not worth the making. Your fears are more numerous than at any other part of your cycle.

5. When you reach the mid-point of your mood cycle, that is the time you make your best decisions. You are not blinded by the glitter of the crest nor disheartened by the darkness of the trough. You are more realistic at the mid-point in analyzing yourself than at any other time.

6. Your characteristic mood cycle begins to establish itself in your childhood. By the time you reach adolescence, it is fairly well set. From then on it doesn't change much *unless you take steps to change it.*

7. If you wish to change it—if you wish to make it conform to *type C, the mature,* here is what you do:

*First,* plan your mood cycle so that you can anticipate the recurrence of your crests and troughs. To do this, take a piece of graph paper and number the columns at the bottom of the page. These numbers refer to days. At the left-hand margin write down the following words in a column thus:

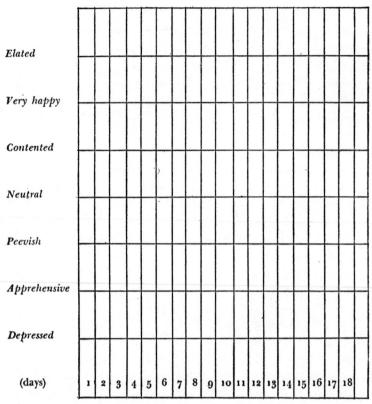

At the *same* time every day, say at eleven in the morning, put an X-mark opposite the word that best describes the way you feel at that time. Continue to do this every day for at least 60 days; 90 days is better. At the end of that time connect all the X-marks with a continuous line. This line will describe your mood cycle in a fairly accurate way.

*Second,* study your mood cycle. How many crests do you have in a 90-day period? How many troughs? Which are more frequent? Which last longer?

*Third,* mark on your personal calendar when you expect your crests and troughs during the next six to twelve months.

*Fourth,* anticipate the troughs particularly. As they approach, remind yourself that they will pass. Minimize their effects by scheduling invigorating exercise, happy companionship, inspirational reading, and easy tasks for the duration of the downswings and troughs.

These things will stimulate you so that you will not feel as depressed or fearful as if you did nothing but commiserate.

For example, a writer I know schedules the planning of a new article or book for his crests. He reads proof during his troughs. Reading proof is easy for him. It doesn't call upon his creative powers. Because it is easy to do, it gives him a sense of accomplishment and thus helps to lessen the pangs of his depression.

A salesman I know increased his sales by a large margin after he planned his calls according to his mood cycle. When his mood is on the upswing he calls on his tough customers. When he experiences a *trough,* he calls on those customers who always renew their orders. Result is, he feels successful on the days of his gloom! And this takes the edge off his depression.

In summary then, each one of us can make our knowledge of fear pay dividends. Our first duty to ourselves is to improve constantly our habits of health. For when we are healthy we are in the best condition to ward off fear and its aftereffects.

The second thing we can do is to make use of our knowledge of the physiology of fear. After a fright, we will now work off the excess sugar in the blood stream by exercising. If, for example, you are beset by fear of losing your job on a blue Monday, take a vigorous walk after leaving the office. Your body will then be in better shape when you sit down to dinner. Your sleep will then be more restful that night.

Third, analyze and study your mood cycle. Take well-defined steps to make it conform as much as possible to Type C.

Expect to spend a lot of time on this, particularly if your present mood cycle is of long duration. The sustained effort will be richly rewarding.

By taking such steps as these we gain victory over fear. For after all, we can demonstrate through patient attention to details that we are masters of our fate and captains of our souls.

# 3. Talk Yourself Out of Your Fears

IF YOU HAVE NEVER TALKED to yourself in the right way, I invite you to take part in a simple experiment. You will enjoy it.

You will find so much happiness in the experiment that you will remember it as long as you live. For it will unlock great personal power now bottled up within you. It will help you triumph over your fears.

Simply repeat the following words out loud. After each sentence, pause to let the meaning sink in:

"The words I am about to utter are going to remain fixed, imprinted, and impressed in my mind. They will remain fixed, imprinted, and impressed in my mind, so that without my will and knowledge, without my being aware of what is taking place, I and my whole organism will obey them.

"First, every day, three times a day, morning, noon and evening, at mealtime, I will be hungry. That is to say, I will feel that pleasant sensation that makes me think and say 'My, but I'm hungry.' I will then eat with a hearty appetite. I will enjoy my food. But I will never eat too much. I will eat just

33

the right quantity for me. Not too much; not too little—just enough for me, I will know intuitively when I have had enough. I will chew my food thoroughly. I will transform my food into a smooth consistency before I swallow it. In this way I will digest my food well. I will feel no discomfort of any kind either in my stomach or intestines. I will digest and assimilate my food perfectly.

"My body will make the best possible use of the food to make healthy, strong muscle and bone, abundant energy. I will eat a wide variety of nourishing foods. If, up to the present, I have been a squeamish eater, I will henceforth eat with enjoyment all wholesome, well-prepared foods. As I eat, I will take joy in and give thanks for food, eating, and my good appetite.

"Since I have digested my food rightly, my excretory functions will take place normally. My bowels will move every morning immediately after getting up and without any laxatives or any artificial means. My kidneys and bladder will do their work thoroughly.

"Every night I will fall asleep at the time I wish. I will continue to sleep until the hour I want to arise next morning. My sleep will be calm, peaceful, deep. I may dream, but all my dreams will be pleasant ones. On waking up I will feel well, energetic, alert; eager to get started on my day's work. Going to bed and getting up will be happy experiences.

"If I have in the past been depressed or filled with gloom, fears, vague forebodings or worries, I will henceforth be free of such negations. Instead of being depressed, fearful, and anxious, I will be cheerful, happy, optimistic. I will be happy without a particular reason, just as in the past I was unhappy without real reason. Henceforth I will be happy. Even if a serious problem should arise in my life, I will not be depressed. For I know that my happy frame of mind will be able to cope successfully with whatever I face.

"If I have been unkind, short-tempered, or impatient, I will no longer be so. Rather, I will be kind, self-controlled, and patient. The things that used to irritate me will leave me wholly calm and self-possessed.

"If I have allowed my mind to dwell on evil or unwholesome thoughts, fears and phobias, I will no longer give them a place in my mind. I will see them vanish like steam in the air. They will no longer be a part of me.

"I will always know that my organs function perfectly. My heart beats normally. My circulation takes place as it should. My lungs work regularly and well. My stomach, bowels, kidneys, gall bladder, liver, bladder, sinuses—all work efficiently. If any of my organs is out of order the condition will grow less day by day, so that shortly it will have disappeared entirely and the organ will have resumed its right and normal function.

"If I am under the care of a physician I will co-operate with him. I will follow his orders. I will take his medicine and treatments regularly. I will speed up their effects through right thinking.

"If there is an injury in any organ in my body, from this time it will gradually be repaired, and in a short time it will be restored completely. I know this will be so even if I should be unaware that the injury exists.

"When I have any task to perform, I will always think that it is easy. I will rule out words, such as 'hard,' 'I can't,' 'impossible,' 'difficult.' In their place I will put 'It is within my power to do,' 'It is easy,' 'I can do it.' By considering my work easy, even though others may say it is difficult, I will find it actually easy to do. For I will do it easily. I will do it without fatigue; in an effortless way.

"In my dealings with others, at home and on the job, I will be happy. My attitude toward others will be kindly and helpful. I will always give the other fellow the benefit of all doubts that may be raised against him. I will embrace the affirmative frame of mind.

"I will expect the best from others. I will be kind and considerate. I will use words of reason and praise. I will control my temper. For I am a mature person.

"If in the past I have lacked confidence in myself, I will henceforth have confidence in myself. My confidence will grow daily, for it is based on the knowledge of the immense power within me. This immense power within me will allow me to accomplish any task of which my common sense approves. With this confidence I will be able to do anything I wish to do, provided it is reasonable and is my duty to do.

"Last, I will rid myself of all fear. I will never again allow myself to be the victim of anxiety, dread, or worry. I will govern my life henceforth by facing my problems squarely. I will use constructive thinking. I will use direct action, rather than procrastinate. I will stop all whimpering, complaining, and self-pity. I will keep my promises. I will think thoughts of courage. I will do courageous actions, I will henceforth be unafraid— For I now realize and will continue to do so as long as I shall live that I will have more health, more happiness, more wealth, more love and affection in my life. I have found a way to abundance and happiness. I will henceforth practice only affirmative thinking. Because I am, I can. Because I can, I will."

Now you feel better. You feel a new courage. Even if you are healthy, wealthy and wise, you feel stronger, better for having said aloud to yourself the powerful affirmations.

If you have a patch of gray at the temples, you are old enough to remember the famous saying, "Every day in every way, I am getting better and better." It was the rage, back in the twenties, as was its author, Emile Coué of Nancy, France.

This remarkable old man did a lot of good. He himself helped thousands of sick, crippled and fearful people to health and courage simply through his teachings of induced *autosuggestion,* as he called it.

Some of the greatest physicians of Europe and the Americas lauded him and his work. Actually, they often sent him a patient beyond their powers of diagnosis and cure. You will remember that Coué was originally a pharmacist who became interested in the psychology of the subconscious mind. He wrote a small, influential book, *Self-Mastery.* Eventually he turned his home and garden into a clinic, where the afflicted congregated from everywhere. He began each session of his clinic by making general suggestions to the group, such as you have just repeated. Many of his ideas are found there.

One example from Coué's records will do:

A physician sent Coué a male patient of about forty years of age. This man had been confined to his room for more than a year, bedridden for the most part. One day, about five months before Coué first treated him, the patient was seized at five o'clock with a violent paroxysm of dyspnoea (shortness of breath). He imagined from moment to moment that he was dying. Various remedies prescribed by the doctor failed to give him relief. The crisis continued until half-past nine in the evening. Next day the patient said to his wife towards half-past four that the paroxysm would shortly recur. When the clock struck five, the dyspnoea returned in full force, passing through exactly the same phases as before and subsiding at half-past nine. Henceforth, the crisis recurred daily *without exception* for five months.

"When he arrived at the clinic I asked him to take a seat, and watch what was going on," Coué states. "I began to make general suggestions to them. I next proceeded to make appropriate suggestions to each patient, and told him to return next day at the same hour. When he kept his appointment, I asked him how he was. 'I had no paroxysm,' he answered. 'I knew I should be all right yesterday when I left you.' Further suggestions were made that afternoon, and a fresh appointment was arranged for the morrow. At this third visit, the report was the same. The paroxysmal dyspnoea was cured, and has not since returned."

The patient's first attack was doubtless genuine, brought on by physical disturbance. Those that followed, he brought on himself by *expecting* the trouble to recur at the customary time. He had *suggested to himself* that the symptoms would return. But just as soon as he affirmed that they would not recur, they ceased! And this is the important lesson: we can use suggestion to bring on disease and fear. Or, we can use it to bring us health and serenity.

Coué's teachings are of course not new. They were old in Socrates' day—Socrates who lived almost 2,500 years ago. Jesus of Nazareth used affirmations. He induced positive suggestion in the halt and blind he cured. As soon as they *believed* they would walk and see, they did! Theirs was a sublime faith, inspired by the teachings of the greatest healer of all time.

All great healers have discerned the power in positive suggestion. To be sure, they use various names: self-direction, autosuggestion, positive thinking, attitudinal therapy, affirmations, etc. But all these are essentially one and the same. Affirmations, then, are valid assertions that you and I direct toward self-improvement. They are "yes" rather than "no"; "I can," not "I can't" or "I doubt." To say "I will *try* to do so and so" . . . smacks of doubt; to say "I will do so and so" is much better. Napoleon once came galloping up to a young lieutenant and said, "Can you take yonder hill?"

"Sire," was the immediate response, "I can try."

"Any fool can try! Can you do it?" snapped back the Emperor.

"Did you ever hear of a man," writes Henry David Thoreau, "who had striven all his live faithfully and singly toward an object, and in no measure obtained it? If a man constantly aspires, is he not elevated? Did ever a man try heroism, magnanimity, truth, sincerity, and find that there was no advantage in them—that it was vain endeavor?"

Captain Eddie Rickenbacker tells us, "As I roared down the last stretch in an auto race years ago, I felt I could control that machine with my mind, that I could hold it together with my mind, and that if it finally collapsed I could run it with my mind. It was a feeling of complete mastery, of supreme confidence. But it was real."

Of course if he had said such a thing at the time, his friends would have called him crazy. He says, "Even now I can't explain it. But I believe that if you think disaster, you will get it. Brood about death and you hasten your demise. Think positively and masterfully, with confidence and faith, and life becomes richer in achievement and experience."

Eddie Rickenbacker's career is an amazing testimonial to his belief in affirmation. He says, "Perhaps such things as the control of mind over matter and the transmission of thought waves are tied up together, part of something so big we haven't grasped it yet. . . ."

Suppose Jane Frohman, the Broadway star, had accepted the verdict that she would probably never walk again, after her smash-up in an airplane. She would not have walked. But she affirmed that she would walk. She held on to that idea as she exercised. And as you know, she eventually took her rightful place again in the theater.

Or suppose the lovely Kyle MacDonnel of television fame had been convinced that she would never leave the tuberculosis ward she was sent to as a high-school girl. Suppose her thoughts had dwelt on dying. As a result of her *will-to-live* she was, two years later, (a) featured in Max Gordon's *Park*

*Avenue,* (b) presented with three movie offers and (c) mistress of ceremonies of her own television show. She had not only regained her health; she had achieved extraordinary success through her affirmations.

The countless cases of disease and poor health corrected by affirmation should put us on guard against symptoms or aches and pains the physicians can't account for. Mrs. A—— always gets a migraine headache on the day she entertains. John B—— is seized with a dizzy spell every time he goes away on a business trip. When Mary C—— is tired she gets a toothache that disappears as soon as she calls the dentist for an appointment. (Incidentally, he finds no cavities.) Mrs. D—— develops asthma every November. It disappears just as soon as she goes to Florida.

In every one of these five cases, the symptoms disappeared with the practice of affirmations. There was no physical cause. Each person had, for his individual reasons, clung to his symptoms for a purpose.

Here is another experiment, first described many years ago by the French savant Chevreul. (He lived to be a hundred.) Take a piece of string a foot long. Tie a key (or some other small metal object) to one end of the string. Now hold the other end of the string between the thumb and forefinger of your preferred hand, with the elbow resting on a desk (or table). Lean over the desk, and bring your thumb and forefinger close to but not touching your forehead. As soon as the key hangs steadily, think of it swinging like a pendulum: to and fro . . . to and fro. . . . Concentrate on its swinging like a pendulum, and eventually it will move like that. On the other hand, if you say to yourself, "All right, swing like a pendulum. I dare you to. You've got to show me. I'm carrying out the directions. Go ahead, swing."—of course the action won't take place. Why? Because you are negatively disposed.

Rest a minute or two. Then hold the string as you did before, and think of the key swinging forward and backward. Again it will follow your concentration. After another rest period, hold it as before and think of the key as describing a circle. Again it will follow the suggestion you send out.

Whenever you isolate an idea in your mind and concentrate on it, and wish to dominate it—the idea takes the form of suggestion. The suggestion makes your body react. Always remember a basic psychological law: *the body never acts; it only reacts*. That is why the fearful person is tense and has bodily ailments. The negative ideas he concentrates on are translated into negative bodily reactions. His ideas give him a haunted look, tense postures, a spastic alimentary canal, or ulcers and so on.

Imagine twin sisters both suffering from anemia. The same physician treats both sisters with the same kind of medicine. One sister believes in the doctor. The other does not. One sister takes the medicine with the positive suggestion that it will help her. The other sister doubts its efficacy. Which sister gets well quicker?

You see therefore, how necessary it is for us to concentrate on positive, rather than negative, thoughts. You can appreciate how a man who says he would like to be wealthy, *but who always expects to be poor,* loads the dice in favor of poverty. He is like the one who goes through the motions of holding the key close to his forehead but doubts that it will swing in unison with his suggestion. Our foolish fellow says to himself, "Wouldn't it be fine to be rich? But pshaw, what's the use? I'm meant to be poor. I'll be lucky if I can make ends meet."

Or take the hypochondriac who tells you he would give anything for good health and then dwells on his imaginary aches and pains. Until he suggests to himself good health, energy, keen appetite and excellent digestion, he will remain a hypochondriac. Until he shifts the focus of his attention from imaginary symptoms of illness to thoughts of health, he will stay fear-ridden about disease. For attention to pain increases it.

And contrariwise. When you shift your attention from pain to wholesome thoughts you decrease it. Winfred Rhoades in his excellent book, *The Self You Have To Live With,* tells about when St. Francis of Assisi had a wound extending from his right eye down the length of his chest. It had to be cauterized. Those were the days before anesthetics.

Listen to the saint approach his ordeal. "My brother Fire, noble and useful among all other creatures, be kindly to me in this hour, because formerly I have loved thee, but I pray our Creator who created us that He will so temper Thy heat that I will be able to sustain it." The saint then relaxed and centered his attention on healing. He focused his attention constructively. After the ordeal he invited the surgeon to cauterize it again, since he had felt no pain.

"Ah yes," you say, "but I am not a saint."

We have only to turn to the modern miracle of painless childbirth without pain to demonstrate the power of affirmations. Dr. Grantly Read, author of *Childbirth Without Fear,* reports that once the pregnant woman learns to relax the muscles of her body, learns also to direct her attention to positive suggestion—when her time of delivery comes the birth process is actually painless. No anesthetics are necessary. The laboring mother makes use of the same principle of psychology that St. Francis of Assisi applied.

Try another experiment. You now feel as if you are going to yawn. You recall how puppies and dogs relax when they yawn; how they open their mouths wide as a barn door. You think of the person in your acquaintanceship who yawns more often then anyone else you know. You feel your own soft palate raise, your lips apart. You catch the delicious intake of relaxation. Think of it. Visualize it. Are you yawning?

Your hair is well combed. You shampoo it regularly. But now, as you think of it, your head itches. Scratch it a bit. It itches more, doesn't it?

These simple experiments show us that when we concentrate on "the feel of" a sensation, the sensation actually tends to take place. You can therefore bring on sensation, either of pleasure or pain, at will. Take your choice. It is up to you.

As in the experiment with the key on the end of the string, the *idea* of movement actually brings about the desired movement. The muscles of your body obey your suggestion without your consciously moving them. Psychologists have known for a long time that every idea you hold tends to be transformed into action. A man says to himself, "I never seem to get out of life what others get out of life. The truth is, my abilities are mediocre. I'd like to be free of fears, but I've lived too long with them. I will always have them. . . ."

When he suggests such negative ideas to himself, he helps to make them materialize. He may work hard, but his work is full of errors. He may strive with others for promotion, but he brings his mediocrities to the fore with his doubts. Under such a negative caste of thought, success and freedom-from-fear elude him. Until he changes his thought-ways! Then watch things change!

Jane E——, nice-looking and twenty-six, came to take some aptitude tests. She had tried two jobs in different fields, unsuccessfully. In the interview we asked her about marriage. We wanted to know whether she was seeking a permanent career or a stopgap job. "I'll never marry," she said, "I'm afraid of it; men are untrustworthy. Anyhow, divorce and heartbreak are the rule. Men are selfish. They live by a double standard . . . ," etc. Her negative attitude must certainly have scared away good marital candidates from her door. With right thinking she could make a wonderful marriage.

The other day I gave the Rorschach Diagnostic Test to a woman beset by many fears and hatreds. Perhaps you know this test as the "ink-blot test." Ten cards comprise the test. On each of the cards are ink blots. The subject tells the psychologist what he sees—what the ink blots mean to him. Of course they are simply ink blots; and each subject projects what is in his imagination. When I showed the woman the fifth card she screamed and threw it across the room. "Rats, rats! Oh, please don't ever show that to me again. Don't ever mention the word *rats*. I'm scared to death of them. I keep them out of my mind. I'd die if I'd see one run across the floor!" Evidently she was sincere, for she wept and showed great agitation. (Notice all the negations she uttered.)

It took a long time to get her to adopt the suggestion that rats are part of the scheme of the world. That she will not likely meet them. That pictures of them are harmless. That rats run away unless cornered. That she has no need to fear them. Once she made suggestions of that sort to herself, she looked at pictures of rats with equanimity. She no longer fears them. Through affirmative suggestion, she triumphed over a painful fear.

And so, by holding the positive attitude, by affirming health, competence, wealth, happiness, poise, friendships, courage, love and affection—we can encourage these things to come our way. They are within you—just for the asking. Talk to yourself with affirmations, and the good things in your life will multiply. And fears, doubts, and worries will leave you.

Love and kindness and generosity spring from within. They are attitudes nurtured by talking to yourself. They are a ready-made foresight buried in the conscience. They are a kind of simple wisdom that anyone can use if only he has the wish to do so.

# 4. Devote a Part of Each Day to Contemplation

IN THE TWENTY-FIFTH YEAR of our marriage, my wife and I spent Christmas week end at a resort not far from New York. As we drove into town we passed the Friends Meeting House. "Have you ever been to a Quaker meeting?" one of us asked. As neither of us had, we resolved to attend the Friends Christmas service.

The next morning, we entered the meeting house shortly before eleven and sat down among the small congregation. We were struck by the simplicity of the place: no choir loft, no pulpit; no organ or stained-glass windows. All the pews were arranged in the usual way except one of them. This pew was on a low dais and faced the others. Two elderly gentlemen sat on this elevated pew.

At eleven, the two old men bowed their heads in silence and the congregation did the same. Nothing happened for about a half-hour. Nothing except profound silence. And then one of the old men stood up and spoke. He said, "I feel moved to tell the story of the Great Stone Face."

He recounted Hawthorne's famous tale of the White Mountains: how long ago, one afternoon when the sun was going down, a mother and her little boy Ernest sat at the door of their cottage, talking about the Great Stone Face.

"The Great Stone Face was a work of Nature in her mood of playfulness, formed on the perpendicular side of a mountain by some immense rocks, which had been thrown together in such a position as, when viewed at a proper distance, precisely to resemble the features of the human countenance. . . . There was the broad arch of the forehead, a hundred feet in height; the nose, with its long bridge; and the vast lips, which if they could have spoken, would have rolled their thunder accents from one end of the valley to the other. . . .

"It was a happy lot for children to grow up to manhood or womanhood with the Great Stone Face before their eyes, for all the features were noble, and the expression was at once grand and sweet, as if it were the glow of a vast, warm heart, that embraced all mankind in its affections, and has room for more. It was an education only to look at it. According to the belief of many people, the valley owed much of its fertility to this benign aspect that was continually beaming over it, illuminating the clouds, and infusing its tenderness into the sunshine. . . .

" 'Mother,' said Ernest while the Great Stone Face smiled on him, 'I wish that it could speak, for it looks so very kindly that its voice must needs be pleasant. If I were to see a man with such a face, I should love him dearly.'

" 'If an old prophecy should come to pass,' answered his mother, 'we may see a man, some time or other, with exactly such a face as that.'

"And then she recounted how, at some future day, a child should be born hereabouts, who was destined to become the greatest and noblest personage of his time, and whose countenance in manhood, should bear an exact resemblance to the Great Stone Face. . . .

" 'Oh mother!' cried Ernest. 'I hope I shall live to see him!' And Ernest never forgot the story his mother told him, throughout his boyhood and when he became a man. . . .

"Rumors went throughout the valley from time to time that the great man who was to bear resemblance to the Great Stone Face had appeared at last. First, there was Mr. Gathergold who returned to the valley after many years of fortune-building. He built himself a huge palace, and the people welcomed him with, 'The very image of the Great Stone Face!' But Ernest saw that his face was a sordid one.

"Later on, the people thought that Old Blood-and-Thunder, the famous general, must surely be the reincarnation of the Great Stone Face. But Ernest sighed, 'This is not the man of prophecy.'

"The years sped on. Ernest was now in the middle years. And again a famous man returned to his birthplace—Old Stony Phiz, a candidate for the Presidency. The crowd yelled, 'Huzza for Old Stony Phiz! There! Look at Old Stony Phiz and then at the Old Man of the Mountain, and see if they are not as like as twin brothers!' But Ernest saw not the likeness; neither, in time, did his neighbors.

"As the years sped on Ernest's faith in the prophecy increased even as the whiteness of his hair. 'Lo, here I am, Ernest!' the benign lips seemed to say. 'I have waited longer than thou, and am not weary. Fear not; the man will come.'

"One day a famous poet stopped at Ernest's door for shelter. Ernest had read his poems and hoped the prophecy would be fulfilled in the poet. Again he was disappointed. As he walked with the poet they met a group of villagers. And Ernest talked with them about the simple thoughts within his heart. At that moment, in sympathy with a thought which he was about to utter, the face of Ernest assumed a grandeur of expression, so imbued with benevolence, that the poet, by an irresistible impulse, threw his arms aloft and shouted, 'Behold! Behold! Ernest is himself the likeness of the Great

Stone Face!' Then all the people looked and saw that the prophecy had been fulfilled. . . ."

After telling the story the old Quaker said, "As a man thinketh, so is he." And then he sat down and bowed his head.

Perhaps ten minutes went by before a man stood up in the congregation, and said, "During the past week I have given a great deal of thought to what is an obvious injustice in our community. As you know, a large part of the population of our town is colored. These people serve our hotels and resorts. They carry a good deal of the local tax load. Yet, I find that not one colored girl has ever been accepted in the nurses training course in our city hospital—not one colored interne has been allowed on the staff. I believe that God would not like us to permit this injustice to continue. I invite you to join with me this week in devoting a portion of your daily contemplation and prayer to this problem. Let us ask for Divine Guidance, so that we may do something constructive about it."

Then he sat down. Again heads were bowed until the town hall clock struck twelve. Then, the two old gentlemen shook hands, and the meeting broke up.

I have attended Gothic Cathedrals, beautiful synagogues, rich and handsome churches. I have been to revivals; to all sorts of religious service: Unitarian, Christian Science, New Thought, Theosophy, Seventh-Day Adventists, Presbyterian, and others. But none of them was ever so impressive as the simple meeting of the Friends on that Christmas morning. Here was deep quiet; contemplation that ended only when someone felt the impulse to share the message of his heart. It inspired. It lead to right thinking. It deepened the knowledge of Self. It turned attention to things of the spirit as well as things of the world.

In addition to their love of peace and their commitment to live by the Golden Rule, the Friends make much of silence in their individual lives—every day. Their religion is actually a way of life. It isn't practiced only on Sunday. It infuses everything they do.

They speak of two kinds of silence. By *dead silence* they mean idle daydreaming, when vagrant thoughts clutter up the mind. Dead silence they neither admire nor practice. It had best be spent in sleep, they say.

By *living silence* they mean communion with oneself. It is a dynamic thing. It brings peace to the heart. It lends purpose to one's life. It helps spread serenity where we live and work. It relaxes us; makes the spirit alive and fresh. It dispels the vague uneasiness and worries that plague most of us who have "nothing higher to hold on to." It allows time for self-study. It increases our perspective; deepens our insight; helps one to put first things first. You may call it prayer, if you wish. Certainly it is a magnificent way to vanquish fear.

You can't deny that the Friends have a successful way of life. They are long-lived, for they practice moderation. Poverty is virtually unknown among them. They help one another. All during the great depression no government doles were accepted by members of Friends. They took care of their own. You perhaps know about the great program of charity and rehabilitation they brought to postwar Europe. I know of no religious group more destitute of fear than the Friends. As a psychologist, I attribute this to their habit of *living silence,* and what comes out of it.

Since that memorable Christmas service with the Friends, I have tried to spend a part of each day in living silence. When I am traveling and cannot find a quiet corner for contemplation, I feel impoverished. Perhaps you already devote some time each day to living silence, contemplation, or quiet prayer. If you do, you already know the vast benefits that follow from it.

If, on the other hand, you have not tried it, you may want to begin now. If you don't know how to begin, why not recall what the Bible tells us to do: "When thou prayest, enter into thy closet, and when thou hast shut the door, pray to thy Father, which is in secret; and thy Father, which seeth in secret, shall reward thee openly."

May I tell you how one man goes about it? He usually awakens at six in the morning. Three quarters of an hour later he is ready to go to work. But as he doesn't have to leave home to catch the train to the city until seven, he seeks out a quiet corner where he can be alone. Then he devotes fifteen minutes to living silence.

Ordinarily, he begins with a short silent prayer. If a prayer of his own isn't forthcoming, he repeats the Lord's Prayer or the Twenty-third Psalm. A formal prayer, uttered in silence, helps him to get in the right frame of mind. He then thinks thoughts of gratitude for his many blessings: health, family, home, work, friends. Then he asks that insight and peace of mind be given those friends and clients who have shared their sorrows with him. He mentions silently their names with the request that their understanding, even as his, be deepened. He proceeds to think of the leaders of the nations of our world and directs to them the thought that they shall have strength and understanding to keep peaceful and constructive ways. He particularly singles out those leaders who obviously are pursuing negative ways; ways of hatred and violence—and asks that they may endorse affirmative and wholesome policies.

He then asks that blessings be showered on those who seemingly have done unkindnesses to him and his. If he is faced with a fear, he analyzes it. He does the same with a personal problem. He tries to divest the problem of emotional entanglements; he tries to think it through—to find out what is the *right* course to follow. He usually ends the fifteen-minute period with an appeal for strength and understanding to do a good day's work.

I mention these details simply as the course one man found easy and helpful to follow. You may wish to do the same. Or, you may want to use a different approach. Your problems, as you see them, may call for a shift in emphasis. The important thing is to get in the habit of spending a few minutes every day in living silence. Some days you will experience a much closer feeling to the Divine Power than on others. Rude and negative thoughts will be easier to keep out of mind some times than at others. But if you build the habit, your ability to concentrate on positive thoughts will grow.

You may find in the beginning that you need to spend all your time asking for personal guidance or favors. If you believe that your life is impoverished of love, money, or health, you may need to concentrate on your many blessings. Don't say, "Do I have any?" For you have many. Yes, everyone has. We are as a lot, we human beings, often ingrates. We forget what we have, in our eagerness to get more. As the old hymn goes, "Count your many blessings, name them one by one." It is excellent psychology. Time and again I have observed a man take a new tack toward success just as soon as he gave up bewailing his fate and thought about his blessings. One's daily periods of living silence are good times to count and bless what we have.

As you grow in living silence, your generosity will force you to think increasingly of others. Your attention will turn to those who need your good wishes and prayers: men and women you work with; those whose sorrows you may know about, even though they may be strangers to you personally.

You will notice a new lightness in your heart, a quickened pride in yourself, as the results of this selflessness. For they will benefit from your positive thoughts.

The great poet Tennyson tells us in *The Idylls of the King*, "more things are wrought by prayer than this world knows of." You probably would be amazed if you could know the number of people you come in contact with who think wholesome thoughts about you. Yes, people who actually pray for you. This, to me, is one of the meanings of Tennyson's line.

Perhaps the next step of growth in your living silence will be thoughts directed to the betterment of the world. The atomic era has brought us closer together than ever before. We feel the intimacy of our neighbors on the other side of the globe. A bomb in Korea actually echoes in Ohio. We know that our leaders in all the nations must become wiser, more kindly, filled with greater concepts of love—if we are to survive. For our intellects have brought forth all sorts of engines of destruction. We need larger hearts, deeper insight, to keep those destructive elements in check. And so, our world leaders need the positive thoughts and prayers of all of us.

The most difficult step to take, of course, is to think kindly and constructively about those who wrong us. Our natural inclination is to strike back; to wish our enemies ill. The ability to think kindly about one who has treated us shabbily—yes, to wish him well—is perhaps the highest kind of self-control. It is hard work. But once we forgive and go further—actually wish our enemies good fortune—we have a nobility within us that we can get in no other way. Once you can do that, you are beyond the reach of fear. For you then have control of yourself as only the highest developed individuals have control. You are really mature.

Living silence then—or contemplation, or prayer, whatever you choose to name it—brings us many rewards. It brings peace to the troubled spirit. It brings order to chaotic thoughts. It brings the calm out of the tempest. It renews our faith. It gives us daily courage to do our best. Beyond all else, it gives us victory over fear.

One of the results you will experience if you establish the habit of contemplation is greater happiness throughout the day. You will actually carry the spirit of prayer into all your daily occupations. Your speech, the way you move and act, how you deal with others, your decisions—all will be marked by serenity, self-control, and the absence of excitement. Grace and kindness will infuse your deeds and words. Fear, anxiety, and worry will take an ever-decreasing part in your life.

The reason I recommend getting up early to spend a few minutes alone in the quiet of your room is that the world is such a noisy place these days. Thoreau could run away from it all and live the life of a hermit by his beloved Walden Pond. He could sit and do nothing, like a Buddhist priest who finds peace in total inactivity. Some retire to a monastery and live in Trappist silence. Most of us cannot follow in these ways.

Our world today is harder to escape from than formerly. Wherever you go, you are likely to hear a radio. Even at the beach or in the Maine woods you find the portable radio, and your mind rushes from Korea to the Polo Grounds because you can't help lending your ears to the program.

We are the most stimulated of all the peoples who ever lived on this globe. Perhaps we are overstimulated. Perhaps we pay too high a price for the benefits of overstimulation. Television programs keep our youngsters up too late. Their sleep is disturbed as a result by actual psychological study. We reflect our nervousness, our lack of composure, by the vast quantities of chewing gum we chew; cigarettes we smoke;

liquor we drink. Our lives seem to be dedicated, from crib to grave, to St. Vitus.

And so, I say we ought to do something about it all. One thing we can do is to provide ourselves with a bit of daily living silence, even if it means getting up earlier. Another thing we can do is to seek silent moments throughout the day. Perhaps you may want to try spending your midmorning "break" alone. Between appointments you may be able to spend a few minutes slumped in your chair with your thoughts turned inward. Spend those times as quietly as you can. Don't smoke or read or talk. Be still, and notice what happens. You will be relaxed. You will feel a new lease on life. You will build up courage to tackle the next problem that comes your way.

A third thing you can do is to spend more of your leisure in quiet pursuits. The happiest married couple I know spends at least an hour together every evening reading. They practice one of the sternest tests of companionship; to enjoy quietude together. Can you enjoy a walk with a loved one— in silence? Conversation has its place in the amenities of friendship, of course. But idle chattering often is a sign of nervousness, does very little good to the soul. Perhaps you will enjoy gardening. Here you can commune with nature. If you live in the city you may have to take up stamp-collecting instead. For the stamp album, like the rose, can be a quiet friend. The point is, we need more living silence in our lives and we also need more quiet pursuits.

Rabindranath Tagore, the great Indian philosopher and poet, once told how moonlight encouraged his living silence:

> The evening was lonely for me, and I was reading a book till my heart became dry, and it seemed to me that beauty was a thing fashioned by the traders in words.

Tired, I shut the book and snuffed the candle. In a moment the room was flooded with moonlight.

Spirit of Beauty, how could you, whose radiance over-brims the sky, stand hidden behind a candle's tiny flame? How could a few vain words from a book rise like mist, and veil her whose voice has hushed the heart of earth into ineffable calm?

Izaak Walton, our good friend of the 17th century, ended his great book, *The Compleat Angler,* with a word of wisdom for all of us. Unless a fisherman learns it, he will never amount to much as a fisherman. Walton says, STUDY TO BE QUIET. If you can do that you will have little cause to fear. For silence beggeth understanding. There is a power in positive thinking, and living silence makes it grow.

# 5.   Share Your Fears Wisely

IN THAT DELIGHTFUL MOVIE *Father of the Bride,* the father can't go to sleep. His wife has just told him their young daughter is going to get married. The father rolls and tosses with the fear that she has made a poor choice of a husband. Finally, he awakens his wife, who asks what's the matter.

He tells her they know virtually nothing about their prospective son-in-law or his background. He tells her he's afraid the young fellow may not be able to support a wife; that he may be a crackpot— He mentions a whole string of doubts that beset him.

At that, the wife becomes worried too. When he sees that, he says, "Now I've got it off my mind! You worry about it. I'm going to sleep." And he does.

J. P. McEvoy tells a story about Jake. He was moaning and groaning in his bed one night and his wife said, "Jake, what's the matter?" He told her he owed his next-door neighbor Morris a hundred dollars. The sum was due the next morning, and he couldn't pay up. He was so worried he couldn't sleep. Jake's wife raised the window and yelled across the yard: "Morris! Morris! Wake up!"

When Morris came to the window rubbing the sleep from his eyes, she said to him: "I gotta tell you Jake's worried. He can't sleep. He can't pay you the hundred dollars tomorrow. He hain't got it!" Then she shut the window, turned to Jake and said, "Now go to sleep, Morris can do the worrying."

Jake, like so many other husbands, didn't share his fears and worries with his wife soon enough. For she had a simple solution that never occurred to him.

So many of our personal problems are solved as soon as we share them. Wasn't it Ralph Emerson who said that when we share a sorrow it lessens, when we share a joy it increases?

Isn't it strange that so many married couples fail to share their problems with one another? If you were a clergyman, physician, or consulting psychologist you would have countless examples of unsuccessful marriages to call to mind; unsuccessful simply because the husband and wife failed to share their worries and personal problems with one another.

Perhaps you would be amazed at the number of marriages in which mutual trust doesn't exist between the partners. For example, I'm thinking of a businessman who never tells his wife that he buys stocks. He tells her that business is bad, that she must do with less. He is afraid that she might indulge her tendency to extravagance if she were to know he had money to invest. He complains that his marriage isn't as happy as he hoped it would be. Is it any wonder? For as yet he doesn't understand that one of the foundation stones of a successful marriage must be mutual confidence. Subterfuges always are destructive forces to a marriage. They have a way of insinuating their deadly influence into the most casual and intimate relationships.

Let us assume that this man's wife has a tendency to be extravagant. And let us assume that he wants to help her become more mature in the handling of money rather than lie to her. Isn't it his duty to talk investments over with her in a sympathetic way—to show her how together they must save for a comfortable old age?

His duty also is to make an active partner of her; to help her grow out of extravagance. If after doing this, she fails to co-operate, then she and he together may have to get some help from a counselor. The point is, they must work out a whole-some way of living together in frankness and good will. Oth-erwise their marriage is headed for disintegration, even if they continue to inhabit the same house.

One of the many fine things about working professionally with couples is that we see so many of them develop a suc-cessful marriage, once they face the facts of their problem, tension, or fear. When they do that the rest is usually easy. For there is a way if the will to face the facts and find a solu-tion is shared by husband and wife.

I'm thinking of another case—of the wife who lives in fear that her husband will learn of an old love affair of hers. Her problem is so acute that she is losing weight and can't sleep. Because of her tension, sexual relations with her husband have become unsatisfactory.

Obviously, at least three courses are open to her. First, she can continue to live in dread and face the consequences per-haps of a nervous breakdown. Second, maybe she can learn to throw off her feeling of guilt and decide that she will con-tinue to keep her past hidden from her husband. Then if he should ever learn about it, she can face the problem with him at that time.

Or, third, she can talk the problem out with him at the first favorable time, say within the next week. She may need some help in doing this, perhaps from their clergyman if they are a churchgoing couple.

In most instances of this sort, the third way is the best, for it puts the marriage on a frank footing. Often a crisis of this kind, after the thunder and lightning pass, makes a marriage close-knit, more satisfying to both husband and wife than it was before. It then succeeds in a grand way, particularly if the husband learns the great lesson of forgiveness—doesn't hold a grudge—doesn't make his wife feel guilty—doesn't say, "I forgive you" and then proceed by deed and innuendo to prove that he hasn't forgiven her. For until one has learned the art of forgiveness he has not matured. (Isn't it true that forgiveness often has a way of doing more for the forgiver than for the forgiven?) Such a marriage succeeds in a grand way if the wife makes restitution by kindly actions, and attitudes of sweet maturity.

For whenever we fail to forgive, we imply that we are setting ourselves up as judges of others. "Judge not that ye be not judged" is of course an admonition of deep psychological implication.

So deep, that it and the rest of The Sermon on the Mount is widely recognized today by psychologists as the best testament of psychotherapy. Dr. James T. Fisher, one of America's foremost psychiatrists, in looking back over a long distinguished career of helping people out of their fears and quandaries, writes in his *A Few Buttons Missing: The Case of A Psychiatrist*:*

> If you were to take the sum total of all the authoritative articles ever written by the most qualified of psychologists and psychiatrists on the subject of mental hygiene, if you were to combine them and refine them and cleave out the excess verbiage, if you were to take the whole of the meat and none of the parsley, and if you were to have these unadulterated bits of pure scientific knowledge concisely expressed by the most capable of living poets, you would have an awkward and incomplete summation of the Sermon on the Mount.

* Written in collaboration with Lowell S. Hawlett; published by J. B. Lippincott Co.

In talking about the case of the woman who fears that her husband will learn of her past, I mentioned her need of restitution or expiation.

In all individuals, except psychopathic deviates, idiots, and imbeciles, the sense of right and wrong—the conscience—develops. But the conscience is more than a sense of right and wrong. It is moreover the recognition of the need and also the drive to right a wrong we have committed.

Thus many of our fears are really apprehensions of what restitution or expiation will involve. We are torn between the realization that we ought to right a wrong we have done and the reluctance to pay the price. So long as we bear this conflict within us, we are a house divided against itself. And our self-respect suffers.

This problem of the conscience is so important in relation to an understanding of fears and tensions that we ought to discuss it at some length. Psychologists say that the conscience begins to develop when we are babies, particularly at the nursing stage. We are not born with a sense of right and wrong.

The baby's first object of love is ordinarily its mother. It is she who gives it food and thus makes it feel comfortable and happy. If Baby is breast-fed by a happy mother, so much the better. Baby soon learns to associate mother's smile and loving voice and stroking with approval. This adds up to its first impression of *right*.

Baby also learns to associate frowns, harsh tones, and rejection with *wrong*. Out of these early concepts of right and wrong grow all its future ethical concepts—its conscience.

If Baby is fortunate in having a happy, well-adjusted mother, its sense of right and wrong develops in a wholesome way. In the early years mother will reward it for doing *right*, will punish it when it does *wrong*. By administering rewards and punishment in a consistent and just way, the youngster develops a sense of emotional security.

The hesitant child, the child with difficult behavior problems, is the insecure child—made so by faulty application of rewards and punishment.

Ordinarily, the child of six or seven begins to respond to reason. When he is at this age, the wise mother takes time to explain to him why this action is right and that one wrong. From the beginning she uses praise and other rewards for right actions much oftener than punishment for wrong actions. Why? Because all of us respond better to reward, especially praise, than punishment. For example, a study of kindergarten children proved that they respond better to words of praise than to rewards of chocolate bars! They responded poorly to punishment.

During World War II, it was necessary to train large numbers of inductees to use the Morse Code. Army psychologists worked out lessons on phonograph records which the inductee listened to. Periodically, the recorded voice would say words of encouragement and praise. Controlled experiments proved that the inclusion of such words, "canned" though they were, speeded up the learning time!

The point is that at all ages we respond better to praise (rewards) than to blame (punishment).

To come back to the youngster: As soon as he learns to talk, the wise mother encourages him to share his problems and fears with her. Confident of a sympathetic listener, he runs to her for help with his quandaries. Then she has a wonderful opportunity to develop in him deeper understanding of right and wrong.

One of the lessons she teaches at every opportunity is that mistakes must be paid for. If, for example, at the age of seven he runs across a neighbor's newly seeded lawn after being forbidden to do so, he must make restitution. He may have to give up all or part of his weekly allowance until the repair of the damage is paid for. Once he has made restitution he is praised and showered with affection.

As he matures, he realizes increasingly that to be happy he must pay for his "sins"; sins of omission as well as of commission.

I said that all of us develop a conscience except psychopathic deviates, idiots, and imbeciles. The child born into the world with low intelligence hasn't the capacity to develop the sense of right and wrong except to a very limited extent. It sometimes learns to obey simple rules of conduct without ever understanding their implications.

On the other hand, the psychopathic deviate may have a very high I.Q., but he has a disordered sense of right and wrong. The gangster who can murder in cold blood without feeling remorse is a psychopathic deviate. Stalin is evidently a man of high I.Q., but he has a disordered sense of right and wrong. For example, Winston Churchill reports that at the Yalta Conference Stalin expressed regret that several million Russian peasants had to be "liquidated" in order to advance his program of farm collectivization. Yet he was quite jovial about the whole thing.

Hitler was also of the same stripe. Genocide and other horrors were his tools for getting what he wanted. Upon the occasions of his frightful successes he was reported to be in high glee.

The Stalins and the Hitlers have a sickness of the conscience. While they deserve pity and understanding as human beings, they must be confined for hospitalization at the earliest opportunity, for the welfare of the world. More and more the evidence accumulates that these unfortunate, these psychopathic deviates, lacked the advantages of a happy, guided childhood. Like the typical gangster, their mothers fell down on their job. Usually their fathers did also.

Does the father have a role to play in helping to develop the youngster's conscience? Of course he does. His initial contribution is to help the baby's mother to be a happy, lovable woman. As the baby grows he too has many opportunities to teach lessons of right and wrong. If his standards of child guidance are at variance with his wife's, the youngster is confused. What is right in the eyes of his mother may be wrong from the father's point of view. Or father may be much stricter in matters of discipline than mother. In such a home the mother and father had better resolve their conflicting points of view or their children are headed for serious fears, worries, and tensions throughout their lives.

The happy family shares its problems, fears, and worries. Many parents evidently don't spend enough time at their job of being good parents. Countless children have to seek help outside their homes for the most elementary kind of guidance. Schoolteachers and professors devote many hours each week—in addition to their heavy class schedules—talking over with youngsters their fears and problems. Why? Because mothers and fathers fail to do this. These parents provide their children with good homes, nourishing food, and stylish clothes. But they fall down on the job of being sympathetic listeners and counselors to their children.

Long ago I came to the conclusion that there is no such thing as a consciously, willfully wicked person. When people are wellborn and well reared, they invariably want to do the right thing. But when their insight is beclouded by fear and tension—often going back to their early years—they sometimes make faulty and foolish decisions. And thus they get into trouble.

Through sharing our fears and problems, therefore, we

often get a new perspective. Time and again I have observed a troubled man, woman, or child think his or her own way through a personal problem and come up with an excellent solution, simply as the result of putting his problem into words before a sympathetic listener. Often only an occasional word from the listener, such as "Why?" leads the distressed one to the next step toward a solution. For the conscience can usually be counted on to do its job well, once the fearful one gets the assurance of a sympathetic ear.

To share our personal problems wisely we have to arrange our thoughts. By arranging them we are often forced to put first things first.

The process of ordering our thinking is in itself constructive. It gives us something to do. When we talk out a fear or problem with another we tend to evaluate our reasons. A specious reason that we may accept in the solitude of our room will not stand the test of sharing it with another. And so this procedure of talking out a fear, worry, or personal problem is often a solution in itself.

At least one of the great industrial companies provides psychological counselors to listen to employees who wish to talk out their problems. One woman employee felt highly resentful about the food served in the company cafeteria. She told her "gripe" in infinite detail to the psychologist. As she talked he noticed that she became relaxed. A week later she stopped by his office to thank him. "You know, since I've been to see you, the food is much, much better!"

The psychologist had not done a thing about the food. The chef had not been changed nor the menus. Evidently, the opportunity to get her resentment off her chest with someone in a position of authority was enough to change her attitude. For from then on she was satisfied with her lunches.

Other employees come in to talk about marital problems. No matter what their tension is, so long as they share it wisely they feel better. And thus they are better, more productive employees.

Apparently all of us feel the need at times of a sympathetic ear to drain off our tensions. Speech is a kind of safety valve. But to make it effective we need the right kind of audience. For speech is two-way communication.

We would exclude of course any hysterical sharing of fears. A friend of mine lived in an apartment hotel. One night late he heard the fire alarms. He was on the top floor of the hotel. In the apartment next to him lived a man who had been injured in a war plant. His arm was still in a cast. This man's eighty-year-old mother shared his apartment.

My friend, stepping into the hall, smelled smoke. The man from the next apartment joined him and asked him to help trace it. They did. They discovered that it came up the elevator shaft. Together they pried open the elevator door. The shaft was full of smoke, apparently from burning oil and grease at the bottom.

Meantime, all the other occupants rushed down the stairways to the street. Doors stood ajar. Many people left the building in their nightclothes, and it was winter. The street was packed with a milling, terrified crowd when the fire apparatus arrived.

During this panic my friend and his neighbor turned a fire extinguisher on the flames. Firemen came up the stairs, dragging heavy hose behind them. The first fireman was just in time to see these two put the fire extinguisher down.

Half an hour later two hundred shivering, rather sheepish people filed back into the hotel and up the stairs. These hysterical people had shared their fears—but not wisely. Mass panic takes place suddenly when crowds share their fear without reason.

The two men who extinguished the fire shared their fears wisely. One was thinking of his old mother, the other of his books and papers. Yet they probably feared fire just as much as those who ran. That is, they *respected* fire. They knew its power to burn and destroy. But they also knew fire could be controlled. Together they solved a problem.

Man's greatest asset, perhaps, is his ability to communicate. A lesson learned by one can be communicated to another. The sound of a soothing voice may in itself quiet a fear. For the voice conveys feelings as well as ideas. The unknown frightens and mystifies us. What is unknown to X may be known to Y. If X will share his fear with Y, he provides himself with a possibility of getting rid of it.

One of the most widely used psychological tests these days is *The Minnesota Multiphasic Personality Inventory*. It contains 550 cards. On each card is a statement. The individual taking the test classifies the statements. He sorts them into three classifications: *True, False, Cannot Say*. It is significant that chronically fearful men and women almost invariably classify as *True* the statement, "I cannot tell anyone all about myself." They keep their fears bottled up within them. Once they learn to express them and share them, their fears ordinarily diminish in severity and number.

Those religions that provide for confessions render their communicants a service of mental health. For in the confessional the man or woman can share his sense of guilt—his fear of not being forgiven—with someone who can prescribe a way of expiation. Upon leaving the confessional, the man or woman feels purged of guilt, feels a new courage, a lighter heart.

Psychologists are making good use of *group therapy* to help people to resolve their fears through sharing them. Group therapy—psychologically allied in some ways to confession—is a circle of people led in discussion by a psychologist or psychiatrist. Usually the group is composed of those facing a common problem, such as unresolved fears.

At the first meeting the psychologist may introduce everyone by name. He may then propose a case history for discussion. For example, "Let's have a discussion—an exchange of opinions—during the next hour about Cornelia.

"Cornelia is about thirteen years old and is still wetting the bed. She has been examined by her family physician who reports that he can find no physical cause for her bed wetting. Her kidneys, bladder, and sphincters are all in perfect working order.

"Since there is no physical cause, Cornelia must wet the bed because of a psychological cause, because there are only two over-all causes for bed wetting—physical and psychological.

"Suppose you were faced with the responsibility of getting at the cause of Cornelia's bed wetting; what would be some questions you might ask yourself?"

Someone then proposes that Cornelia may be having trouble in school. Someone else suggests that she is at the age of puberty and may be unduly worried about sex and menstruation. Finally, someone says, "What about her home life?"

At this—now that the ice is broken—the psychologist says, "Those are all excellent leads. As a matter of fact, Cornelia's problem did hinge on her home life. I'd like to tell you what we found out, and then you may want to ask some questions or comment on the case history."

The psychologist then proceeds to point out how Cornelia's parents constantly bickered. Her mother resented the influence of her brother-in-law, her husband's older brother. This man, the oldest of a large family, came to America when he was fourteen years old and eventually built up a big, successful business. He also was instrumental in bringing his family to America and giving them jobs. This man is dictatorial and believes that women aren't men's equals—that their place is in the home—that they should be good mothers, meek and subservient wives.

Now, Cornelia's mother—born and reared in America—was incensed at her brother-in-law's attitude toward women and resented particularly the demands he made upon her husband, who defended his brother.

Cornelia began to imagine that she was responsible for the enmity that existed between her father and mother. These parents tried to "break" Cornelia of bed wetting by all sorts of punishment and also by promising her rewards if she would stop. But to no avail.

The psychologist explained to the parents that Cornelia did not consciously want to wet the bed—that it caused her much feeling of shame. He pointed out that their conflicts made her feel rejected; that she wet the bed in her sleep because subconsciously she wanted to be a baby again. For in babyhood she felt wanted.

He went on to point out that they needed to reassure Cornelia of their affection for her, not only by word but by action as well.

Once the parents understood the cause of Cornelia's problem, they explained to her that they had been wrong, that they loved her very dearly, that she could wet the bed without fear of punishment, etc. From then on Cornelia's bed wetting ceased.

Then the psychologist throws open the case history for comment. Someone asks, "How could they deal with Cornelia's uncle?"

Immediately, someone else offers a suggestion. As the discussion proceeds, individuals begin to tell of personal experiences in their own lives. The psychologist seizes every opportunity to use the comments to deepen insight into the problems faced by the group. As the group becomes better acquainted at successive meetings, the individuals reveal more about their tensions, worries and fears. When this happens they are well on the road to victory over fear. Here again is mission accomplished through sharing wisely.

In many ways the man or woman who has gained victory over fear in his or her own life is in the best position to be a sympathetic listener. Such a person can dispel a fearful one's hesitancy to talk out so-called "foolish" fears. To anyone who has been through the valley of fear there is no *foolish* fear. For we are all such complex creatures—our lives are such intricately woven tapestries—that any one of us might have experienced any fear or phobia. Only the thoughtless or the dim-witted cannot understand that.

And so, with intelligent kindness and abiding sympathy for all, let us every one try to help others share their fears wisely. And also, since charity should begin at home, let us each resolve to share our fears wisely and to share them as they arise.

# 6.   Encourage Those Who Fear

MAY I TELL YOU about Mildred? Just out of high school, she found a job as a stenographer in a Wall Street brokerage house. She had to take down many strange financial terms and abbreviations in her dictation. She was afraid she couldn't make the grade.

The first few days on the job she became tense and jittery, lost her appetite, slept poorly. She felt the job was beyond her depth and that she was a failure. Her great fear was that she might be fired; that she had chosen the wrong vocation.

"I'll bet those new words seem hard," the boss said. "You'll find they get easier day by day. If you'd like to bring me your dictation, I'll be glad to go over the notes to help you with the tough ones." He suggested she draw up a list of each day's new words, and review them. By the end of her first week on the job, he went over the lists and dictated the hardest words for her to take down in shorthand. She got all of them right!

"You were much better than you thought you were, weren't you?" the boss said with a smile. "I've done this before, and your score is just about the best ever!"

Life became a lot more pleasant for her from then on. That's why you said so-long to fear, Mildred. Why you said hello to confidence and joy in your heart.

You can appreciate that Mildred's supervisor is an excellent practical psychologist and also a kind man. The morale of his staff must be sky-high. Encouragement, teaching, reassurance—these are the tools he uses to foster the right kind of human relations. He of course practices the Golden Rule—that cornerstone of right living.

Harold Helfer, the magazine writer, recently pointed out that all the great religions preach the Golden Rule. Their words, as we shall see, vary a bit, but the same idea is embedded in each of their renditions.

### TEN WAYS TO OBSERVE THE GOLDEN RULE

*Buddhism*: "Hurt not others with that which pains yourself."

*Christianity:* "All things whatsoever you would that men should do to you, do ye even so to them: for this is the law and the prophets."

*Confucianism:* "Is there any one maxim that ought to be acted upon throughout one's whole life? Surely the maxim of loving kindness is such— Do not unto others what you would not they should do unto you."

*Judaism:* "What is hurtful to yourself do not to your fellowman, That is the whole of the Torah and the remainder is but commentary."

*Hinduism:* "That is the sum of duty: Do naught to others which is done to thee would cause thee pain."

*Mohammedanism:* "No one of you is a believer until he loves for his brother what he loves for himself."

*Jainism:* "In happiness and suffering, in joy and grief, we should regard all creatures as we regard our own self, and therefore should refrain from inflicting upon them such injury as would appear undesirable to us if inflicted upon ourselves."

*Sikhism:* "As thou deemest thyself, so does others."

*Taoism:* "Regard your neighbor's gain as your own gain: and regard your neighbor's loss as your own loss."

*Zoroastrianism:* "That nature is good only when it shall not do to another what is not good for its own self."

That the ten greatest religions of today should unite in advocating the Golden Rule is proof of its worth to all of us, everywhere.

Broadly speaking, all our unreasonable fears spring from being too self-centered. By thinking more of the welfare of others we have less time and inclination to fret about our own fears. Anything you do to help another, no matter how modest or unheralded, is a contribution to your super-ego's growth.

To the psychologist the super-ego is the highest form of personal development. In a word it is the attitudes and deeds of helpfulness to others. It is unselfishness. When you help a worthy organization raise money for a charity, you exercise your super-ego. When you do kind deeds around home or on the job, you strengthen your super-ego. Every time you think constructive thoughts about others, you also build up your super-ego.

The end result is that you feel secure in the knowledge of your right-doing and right-thinking. Your own fears and worries diminish. You simply haven't time to conjure up selfish hobgoblins. Of the many ways to encourage your super-ego to grow, you will find none more wholesome than the encouragement you give to those with more fears than you have. Ten ways are especially worthy of your attention.

TEN WAYS TO ENCOURAGE A FEARFUL PERSON

1. *Kind words.* Since talk is cheap, why don't we share more of the right kind of it? You will remember as a child how kind words comforted you. The teacher who spoke gently, you always remembered with gratitude. As we grow up, many

of us somehow hesitate to utter the kind words in our hearts. The way to change that is simple. Think how much kind words mean to you. Then you won't be able to stop their flow to others.

The great Roman, Seneca, was desperately ill. Listen to him tell how much kind words helped him back to health:

> My friends have greatly contributed to my cure; their exhortations, their cares, and their conversation have relieved me. You must know, my dear Lucillius, that nothing aids and sustains a sick person like words of affection from his friends; nothing is better fitted to divert his thoughts from the expectation and fear of death. . . .

No matter what your friend's fear may be, if you reassure him with kind words and if you listen sympathetically while he tells you all about it, you provide him with a two-way safety valve. You let him blow off the boiling steam, and you replace it with cool waters.

2. *Sincere voice.* To make the kind words really do their job well, couch them in a sincere voice. The beautiful voice is in itself a soothing thing. If you have never listened to a reliable recording of your voice, you don't know how you sound to others. You will be amazed! In all probability you will want to improve it. A salesman who telephones his lonely wife that he loves her, in a fine voice, does a much better job of reassuring her than in a monotone. Kindly disposed men and women often discover that their voices sound "mushy." Just as soon as they put more vibrancy into their words they do a much better job of reassuring the fearful. I know of no single kind of self-improvement that helps us more than voice cultivation. It does so many fine things for others and boosts our own self-esteem.

3. *Reassuring mannerisms.* Many years ago I worked as a psychologist in a mental hygiene clinic connected with a hos-

pital. Some of the patients were manic, highly excited. The attendant who had the most quieting effect on them was a middle-aged man of little formal education. The psychiatrist would call on him for help. His relaxed facial expressions, his calm, rather slow movements, his gentle voice and smile soothed the patients much faster than all the learning of the specialists.

If you live or work with a chronically fearful child or adult, you will do him a lot of good simply by being a relaxed person. You will of course get rid of all nervous mannerisms, for they are contagious. A pat on the shoulder or a sympathetic nod often do more to pick up flagging spirits than a sermonette. Move more slowly; sit relaxed; smile gently; don't make sudden movements. When you practice such rules you certainly help to spread the sweet contagion of serenity.

4. *Kind deeds.* By being thoughtful we can do many a noble deed without any fanfare. That's what President Harding did on his Inauguration Day. His predecessor Woodrow Wilson, as you know, was a broken man at the end of his eight years in the Presidency. He had borne a terrible burden and thought he had failed. It's the custom at the Inauguration for the President as well as the President-elect to ride side by side to the Capitol. And as they do, they always acknowledge the cheers from the crowd. But Wilson was completely exhausted. When Harding saw that Wilson could hardly lift his hat in response to the cheering crowds along the streets from the White House, he immediately stopped raising his own. In that very important moment of his life, he seemed to forget himself and just to think of the man he defeated. I always think of President Harding's chivalry on his Inauguration Day as an example of how we can spread encouragement by our little actions of nobility.

Most of us don't expect others to give us a million dollars, pay our bills, or send our children through college. We don't anticipate grand displays of generosity. We are grateful for the little thoughtful deeds of daily comfort. If we could multiply them in each life, we would all have fewer reasons to fear. We would have the reassurance of the other fellow's thoughtfulness and affection.

5. *Do what you say you will do.* In helping fearful people we must never break our promises to them, lest we plunge them in despair. Joan, twenty years old, fell in love with her college mathematics instructor. He was five years her senior and a worthy man. He loved Joan and wanted to marry her. When she told her parents, they objected to the match. They wanted her to go to another college. After much unhappiness they promised Joan she might continue at her alma mater, provided she would not marry until she graduated. They also forbade her to become engaged so long as she was an undergraduate.

Joan kept her word. Both she and the math instructor kept the promise. On the day of her graduation, Joan's father told her that he and her mother were taking her to Europe for the summer. On the boat they said they had changed their minds, that Joan would never have their permission to marry her former teacher. She became greatly excited and eventually had a nervous breakdown. Then they were willing to make her other promises "if she would only get well." But she no longer had faith in them.

If you promise a fearful person that you will meet him, don't forget your appointment. If you promise to bring him a book, do it. The fearful one is hypersensitive. Slight transgressions loom large in his mind, increase his doubts, make him lose confidence in you and himself. If you say to a frightened child, "Go to sleep. I promise to stay with you," and he wakes to find you gone, you really let him down.

6. *Write messages.* Is it true that we Americans, because of our telephones and telegraph services, have forgotten how to

write messages of hope and comfort? Of course, a telephone message or a telegram to a friend in need is a good deed. They have their place. But when we use them as substitutes for a "visit on paper," we shirk our duty. Isn't there someone you like very much—beset with fears and worries—who needs a letter from you? How long will it take you to cover one or two sides of a page? Perhaps a nephew is away at boarding school, homesick and miserable. Perhaps you have a friend suffering from cancer, who needs your message badly. You may want to get in the habit of carrying a few greeting cards in your pocket, at spare moments sending off a happy note to a friend or relative needing your encouragement. Let your message be cheerful, full of optimism.

When Abraham Lincoln completed his famous speech at Gettysburg, the audience did not applaud. They were too deeply moved. Lincoln feared that he had failed. How distressed were his thoughts until the letters poured in to reassure him! Every time you write a note of encouragement, you say between the lines, "I think so highly of you that I gladly take the time and effort to write you." Yes, this is surely excellent reassurance for the fearful.

7. *Maintain an even temperament.* Young Henry Ford recently paid a lot of money to Elmo Roper and his associates, the poll-takers, to find out what Ford workers really wanted from their job and company. "Four basic things," reported Roper: " (1) A sense of security. (2) The opportunity to advance. (3) To be treated like human beings. (4) A sense of human dignity that comes from feeling that one's work is useful to society as a whole." Please notice which was placed first: a sense of security.

More and more industrial psychologists are finding that you can't legislate the sense of security among workers. They may have iron-bound contracts to protect their seniority, pay rate, vacations, medical care and hospitalization, old-age retirement, and the rest—yet if the supervisor is cross, sarcastic, or stingy with praise, they lack the sense of emotional security.

If you are a supervisor, a foreman, or any other type of leader, you know how your followers appreciate evenness of temperament on your part. You know also how contagious your calmness is among them. And so it is in all walks of life, wherever groups gather. Those who live their lives on an even plane of feeling, those who don't swing up and down the gamut of emotions, are the really mature men and women. They are the wheel horses that keep the hysterical and fearful a-going.

In the old roundup days on the Texas Panhandle, the buckaroos would drive out a herd of cows from the ranch. Then, when they lassoed mavericks to be taken home, they did something rather strange. They would yoke each wild critter to a domesticated cow. For a day or two, the maverick would pull the poor cow all over the prairie. He'd snort and buck, all full of bile and vinegar. But eventually, the patient cow, by staying calm, would have her own way. She'd bring him back alive, tamed and fit to live with.

8. *Volunteer your help.* Be a good neighbor. "Gossip," said David Starr Jordon, Stanford University's organizer, "is the first art of neighborliness." So don't be afraid to chat in a friendly way with your neighbors. Petty talk—not the vicious kind, of course—has its place in our lives. It helps to cement friendship. It drains off tensions. Use it to put across words of encouragement. Let "Is there anything I can do?" be a favorite question of yours.

A child, deeply perplexed about his homework, may need your help to check his fear of failure. A young mother having to visit a loved one at the hospital may be anxious because there is no one to stay with her boy. The new worker in your department will take heart in his job if he knows you are eager to help him learn the ropes. Be generous. Give yourself away to the fearful. Offer to help.

9. *Appeal to common sense.* Grave fears have a way of paralyzing common sense. They throw things out of perspective. Vincent Sheean in *Not Peace But A Sword* describes a common type of reaction to fear.

> The refugee was a peasant woman. She was complaining of the haste with which she and her family had had to flee. The burden of her complaint was that her husband's new suit and his Sunday gloves had had to be left behind. I had heard exactly the same kind of protest years ago in China; I was to hear it later in Austria and Czechoslovakia. The mind of the refugee, dazed and uprooted, concentrates upon the small, specific losses that it can cling to with understanding. To be homeless and without food or shelter as a result of the "policy" of foreign dictators and prime ministers—that is a state so terrible that it cannot be taken in all at once. The new suit, the Sunday gloves; these are the losses one can still comprehend.

In 1913, I was in Dayton, Ohio, during the great flood. Periodically, the suburbs would get reports, "Flee your homes, the flood is rising!" Those who succumbed to fear left their homes and took with them such useless articles as an empty birdcage, a lamp shade, a roll of piano music. No blankets, food, or medicine. They didn't stop to lock up. Many of them had their houses robbed during their flight. Yet on every street there would be a sturdy soul (or two) who would counsel his neighbors to wait for the reports to be confirmed, or to go down to the water line, and see for yourself." With such common-sense advice he helped many a hysteric to stay or return home.

In all such states of mass hysteria a few words of assurance from you, or a deft question or two, will help the floundering one at your elbow to an even keel again. Make your appeals to common sense strong and persistent.

10. *Divert attention.* Henry Lieferant, the distinguished editor, once told me how the Bolshevik soldiers when they conquered Poland paralyzed whole villages with fire, sword and fear. In at least one village they raped all the nubile women—except one ready-minded lass who knew how to apply the principle of diverting attention. As she saw the soldiers coming, instead of cowering in the cellar like the others, she threw open the door. "Won't you come in and rest while I make you some hot tea?" she said to them with a curtsy. They were so surprised at the unusual reception they didn't molest her. Was she scared? I suspect she was terrified every minute.

A girl in horror at the sight of a rattler will snap out of it when you pass your hand over her eyes. A doctoral candidate, obsessed with the idea he is going to fail his final examinations, may need only your company the evening before they take place, to lift the fear from his heart. Dr. Adolph Meyer, Johns Hopkins University's great psychiatrist, found occupational therapy a cure for many chronically fear-ridden men and women. He distracted their attention from their obsession by keeping them busy: basket weaving, woodworking, the plastic arts, etc.

Oh, you say, but these are rare cases—cases I'm not likely to meet. That may be so. Nevertheless the principle works in all sorts of fear situations, even in the minor fears and worries. You will find that the principle of diverting attention does the trick in your own life. If you are deeply worried, perhaps you ought to go to see a good movie, or play a game of bridge with your friends. See then whether you don't return refreshed, with a better perspective on your problems. For all of us, at times, need harmless escapes from our petty fears.

Weigh these ten ways. Study how specifically you can apply them to those about you. Remember always, they present you with a double opportunity. On one hand, they help ease the burden of others. On the other, they exercise your super-ego, make it grow.

And it is never too late to do this. Think for a moment with me about Marie Antoinette, one of the most beautiful and spoiled darlings of history. Reared as a Hapsburg princess of the proud Austrian Empire, she became the wife of the Dauphin of France. When he was crowned King of France, she ruled over the gayest, most brilliant court of Europe. Versailles and Trianon resounded to her endless soirees and plays. She had more than a thousand party dresses encrusted with pearls, diamonds, rubies, emeralds; more than a hundred white wigs. Her slightest whim was an irrevocable command. Utterly irresponsible—out of touch with the world outside her charmed circle—she is supposed to have said one day, when they told her the people were starving for lack of bread, "Why don't they eat cake?" All the forces of fate had worked to make her grossly self-centered.

Came the revolution. Her husband guillotined. Her only son separated from her. Gone were her ladies in waiting, the flirting, perfumed courtiers. Farewell to the daily banquets of forty-nine or fifty courses! Instead of beauty on every hand, now there was only the rat-infested prison for her. No more fine clothes. Not even a bed. A pallet and a handful of straw for her to sleep on. No one to dress her hair. The warden cropped it off. The mob yelled for her death. They hurled obscenities at her bars. The officials called her "Widow Capet."

But now a miracle of growth took place. She forgot herself in ministering to other noblewomen less courageous than herself. The few letters she was able to smuggle out of the Bastille reflected her new point of view—her sympathy. And finally, when she rode the tumbril she bore herself in simple humility. On the day she was beheaded she was one of the few who mounted the scaffold in proud resignation, unafraid. Her last words were of comfort for others.

Like Marie Antoinette, many of us must face a crisis— although, thank goodness, not such a gruesome one—before we realize the peace of heart that comes only with the self-less attitude. Then, fear bows to our will to help others.

# 7.   Conquer the Fear of Shyness

DO YOU REMEMBER the days of your shyness? The pain you felt? The agony of your timidity? Perhaps you are still shy. Dr. A. A. Roback, the well-known psychologist, finds that 35 per cent of all American adults believe their chief handicap to be shyness or self-consciousness! Think of it, more than every third person believes he's held back by shyness.

Of course all of us go through periods of shyness when we are children. At three years of age and especially during adolescence we feel the pangs of shyness. Ordinarily we outgrow these tough times. Here's how one girl surmounted the problem. I quote from her letter to me, written after she read an article of mine, "Be Glad You're Not Beautiful," in *The American Magazine*, August, 1950; later republished in *The Reader's Digest*.

August 4, 1950

Dear Dr. Bender:

I would like to tell you about a girl friend of mine. . . . Her nose is quite large and she has always been shy and self-conscious of it. For instance, it was rare indeed if she did not shy from a camera, or fail to cover the side of her face when a car passed her on the street. She was, however, a very good reader and started emerging from her cocoon, when her classmates in Junior High School began insisting that she always be the one chosen to read aloud. From then on, she was in the popular girl's club and her marks improved.

A lot of things happened when she was a Sophomore. Her mother died; her grandmother became ill; and her brother went in service. She became a combination house-keeper, nurse, cook, and student but still her marks improved. She took part in all the school plays, earned a gym letter, was an active member of three clubs (officer of two), and baby-sitter and vacation job-holder on the side. She graduated with a B plus average, her grandmother died and brother was killed in an accident—all in the same year.

I see that girl friend every time I glance in the mirror, but I don't feel a darn bit sorry for her. Things can be easily forgotten, and everything above combined to change her from a self-conscious, sarcastic little brat to the better person she is today.

I am almost twenty-one now, married and mother of a five-month-old son. My physical affliction? Well, just before or after we became engaged, I made a remark about my nose. My fiancé stood back and looked at me. "Why it is a little large, isn't it?" he said. He hadn't really noticed! I haven't noticed since then either. To heck with it.

Thank you for the article. It helps to make us average people a little more courageous.

Sincerely,

What a triumphant attitude!

What is shyness in an adult? Isn't it pride? Doesn't it spring from too much self-love? Doesn't the shy person suffer from fear of being ill-judged? Isn't shyness at bottom ignorance of human nature? Isn't it fear of failure to please or measure up?

If you turn your thoughts back upon your adolescent years you may find some facts that never occurred to you then. And if you classify these facts you'll be able to analyze the causes behind your fears. Once you do this, you get a new point of view.

You'll remember being embarrassed when you were a child. Perhaps you hid your face sometimes when you were suddenly spoken to by an older person. You'll remember the rush of blood to your ears and cheeks. You felt a sense of shame. You wanted to escape attention, to pass unnoticed. You didn't want the spotlight turned on you. When someone spoke to you you felt as though a hundred eyes were focused on you, looking through you, able to read your inmost thoughts. You didn't feel secure.

At the earliest possible moment you broke away and ran. Where? It didn't matter. You got away from this imagined concentration of attention. The easiest place to hide was among friends of your own age. You didn't feel embarrassed with them. They were all too busy with their own thoughts and actions to pay close attention to you. They were your own size. You knew them.

Now what caused this feeling of shyness in the presence of your elders? Wasn't it an extreme self-consciousness? Wasn't it an egotistical feeling that you were so important that everyone was listening to hear what you might say? Perhaps you felt they were critical of your appearance. How your hair was combed. And if your hands were clean. Weren't you afraid of being overpowered?

Looking back now you know you weren't under any microscope. There was no reason for you to fear your elders, except that you didn't understand them. (And also, many of them didn't understand you and your quandaries.) You endowed them with powers of penetration which you as a child didn't have. And as you see the picture now it becomes laughable.

Perhaps your hands were dirty. Perhaps you hadn't washed your ears. But these grownups didn't notice that, or if they did, they didn't care. They expected such things of little children. You were giving yourself a terrific importance others didn't recognize. You felt that you didn't measure up to an adult world, and you didn't want these people to find out.

Safe among your own age-group your shyness faded. You felt that they were no smarter than you and you didn't have to pretend. Their standards were yours. If you were shy around your peers, you perhaps played alone too much.

The shyness that characterizes youngsters assumes many forms. It often makes boys into bullies. It isn't normal or healthy for a boy to be a bully, or for a girl to have a domineering attitude. Both of these unfortunate poses result from a feeling of inadequacy, of inferiority. They are brash, unhealthy cover-ups for conditions that can be corrected. These attitudes may be developed by unfortunate conditions in the home of the boy or girl, conditions that they try to hide by assuming threatening, aggressive attitudes. The bully protects his feeling of inadequacy with bluster, by ruffling himself up big.

Such youngsters often develop perspective as they grow up, and overcome the fears that made them tyrants. That is, most of them do. Unfortunately, now and then one continues along the path he set in childhood. Such a person makes no friends. People simply turn away from him. If they mention him at all they say he has an "unfortunate personality."

The objectionable qualities that develop from shyness tend

to sustain fear and doubt. They make for unpopularity. They are the cause of rejection and rebuffs. They put one in a vicious circle.

Other shy tendencies remain in adults, almost like phobias. I have a friend who never had to drive his own car. As a young fellow his father told him he wasn't responsible enough to learn to drive. He had a chauffeur for many years, and came to accept this unusual service as a routine part of his life.

But a day came when my friend met severe financial reverses. He still owned a car. Now if he wanted to go anywhere, he had to drive.

"I used to be afraid of traffic," he told me seriously. "I tried to talk myself out of it, but the feeling of power in that motor made it seem beyond my control. I learned to manipulate the gears and pedals, but I didn't drive the thing. I was a passenger.

"Twice, I tried the test for a driver's license and failed it. I took a grip on myself and said: 'See here, fellow, you've got some brains, and twenty million people in this country drive cars. Surely you're good enough to be one of the twenty millions.'

"I took the test again, and passed it. And I want to tell you that was one of the greatest triumphs of my life. I'm not afraid of autos or any kind of machinery any more. I can make that car do what I want it to do. If only my father were alive, I'd show him."

My friend had been as shy before an automobile engine as a little child before a large group of strangers. Was the motor at fault? No, his fear in his own mind (put there perhaps by his father) had to be conquered in his own mind.

That's a funny thing about fear. You never fear something that you understand. Anything you know and understand you can deal with intelligently. It's always the unknown that creates fear. And fear makes you shy away.

Of course we find many of the unknown things fascinating when they arouse our curiosity without disturbing our safety. That's why mystery stories hold vast reader-audiences enthralled. Mystery stories deal with unknown elements. As soon as the mystery is solved, as soon as the reader becomes aware of all the facts, the story ends. It has to. Once we know all the facts we're no longer interested.

The same thing applies to stories of adventure and big game hunts. When a hunter comes face to face with a tiger, his natural impulse is to run and hide from the unknown quantity, the tiger. Nobody can be sure just what that tiger will do—so the story is interesting until the tiger slinks away into the brush, attacks, or gets shot.

It's the unknown element in a love story that makes it interesting. The elements of shyness and uncertainty in the principal characters create that interest, for two reasons:

(1) They reflect something of your feelings, past or present, toward other people.
(2) They serve to excuse the shyness you have felt at times.

If you were lost in a strange city would you hesitate to ask directions from a stranger? Many people do hesitate to do so. There's no sound reason to be shy of a stranger. Put yourself in his shoes. Wouldn't you help him?

Perhaps you've had the experience of speaking to a stranger, only to have him (or her) turn away and hurry his steps. In such a case, you have no reason to feel embarrassed. Rather, you should be sorry for him, knowing that *he* suffers from the shyness you have long since overcome. Or he may be deaf, myopic, or simply preoccupied. Just ask somebody else. Most people want to help.

Salesmen have to conquer shyness if they're successful. One of the greatest assets any salesman can have is the ability to seem at ease with strangers. If his manner is strained, or his words clipped and short, he brings nervous tension into the conversation and that will damage his persuasion. But if his manner is friendly and confident he creates confidence both in himself and in what he has to sell.

One of America's great salesmen is Harry W. Meyer, Vice President in Charge of Sales of International Cellucotton Products Company, makers of Kleenex, Kotex, and other well-known items. Not long ago Mr. Meyer told me that as a young man he was painfully shy. He couldn't meet people. Yet he wanted to be a salesman. He visited a professor of salesmanship at a great Midwest university. The professor's advice was, "Give up the idea of becoming a salesman. Try something else."

But Harry Meyer's will to be a salesman was too strong to abide by the advice. He said to himself, "My first step is to get over this silly shyness." A little self-analysis told him to begin by looking people directly in the eyes.

Every day he looked steadily into the mirror—for a half-hour at a time. He developed the steady gaze. After practicing this for a long time, he applied it when he talked with others.

He discovered that he was soon using the steady gaze even when he talked with strangers. With this first step accomplished, his confidence grew. Then he developed a more vigorous voice. He put more enthusiasm into his words, more conviction in what he said. Before long he landed a job as a salesman. From then on he rose like a meteor. You may want to adapt Harry W. Meyer's conquest over shyness to your own needs.

One of the outstanding qualities I have noted in successful salesmen is their ability to meet strangers easily, confidently, and to make friends. This ability doesn't lessen the need for a salesman to know his product thoroughly and to believe in it. But knowing his product isn't enough. He can't make a sale unless he's able to answer questions and meet objectives with complete assurance.

The day when the drummer went from store to store through the country, and sold his product on the strength of the stories he had to tell, is past. Yet the assurance with which he approached his customers made him a typed personality. Shyness was a word he didn't understand. He greeted everyone he met as an old friend.

Everyone isn't a salesman by nature. Yet successful salesmen can be made if the will to learn is there. And everyone can learn something from the fact that a salesman is accepted by those he contacts, and that they ordinarily welcome his friendliness.

Have you ever dreaded the "ordeal" of meeting a "perfect stranger" to discuss a business matter? Perhaps you have to talk about a mortgage, or some purchase, or to arrange for postponement of a payment that is due.

Almost everyone has had this feeling of dread in connection with the making of a new contact. I've known young men who actually walked around the block several times before screwing up their courage to enter a business firm for an interview. Under such circumstances it's most unlikely for them to make a favorable impression. Even if the executive they hope to impress tries to put them at ease, he's inclined to consider them unfit for important responsibilities.

It's extremely important for you to conquer the feeling of shyness before you enter the business world in any capacity. Feeling abashed by people affects your thinking. It inhibits the powers within you. It's like a stunning blow that leaves you momentarily helpless; and in business that moment is likely to be an important one, when decisions are made. If a secretary feels shy and embarrassed she's inclined to make mistakes in her work.

Yet when you recognize shyness for what it is, you see how silly it is. Why should you, or any other adult, feel embarrassed or shy in the presence of another adult? Such a feeling doesn't indicate respect. You can't be embarrassed by anyone you think of as a fellow human being. Shyness is an expression of self-conscious opposition to the other person whether or not you recognize that feeling. Everybody has to conquer shyness at one time or another.

A little common sense will tell you that strangers are rarely antagonistic toward you. If the stranger is discerning, your shyness tells him you do not value your own worth. He knows at once that you feel a lack of confidence in yourself and in your abilities. He concludes you are not grown up.

You may protest that this isn't always so. You may feel that you are the master of the subject you're discussing, but shyness makes you hesitate. If you will lose yourself in your subject you'll forget your shyness.

This sense of inadequacy is an experience to be outgrown. There's a period in adolescence when boys and girls are unusually conscious of the development of their own bodies. They are no longer children, not yet adults. They are in the unhappy awkward age. This is a period of clumsiness, of great self-consciousness, a feeling that you are *different* from everyone else. The fear of being overdeveloped, or underdeveloped is very real. Shyness then causes moments of deep embarrassment. It often encourages unusual introversion. Most of us have experienced some of these attributes, but fortunately most of us also develop enough traits of extroversion as compensations before we're out of our teens.

So the shyness people feel before strangers is actually an emotional immaturity. It indicates that they have never outgrown their adolescent fears of inadequacy and self-consciousness. Once they recognize this fact they can put their shyness in perspective to overcome it.

If a midget asks a giant how far it is to the railroad station, the giant's answer will be, "Straight ahead two blocks, then two blocks to the right."

The midget will thank him and go his way with no feeling of fear. A midget *has* to overcome shyness in this world of normal-sized people. And yet there's no feeling of antagonism toward him (or toward a giant). Why should we expect others to feel antagonistic toward us?

All this teaches us some very important lessons, and they're pleasant lessons to learn, simply because they make our lives easier and happier. We have to forget ourselves and become interested in others. We have to be interested in what we have to say if we're to interest others. We have to outgrow the adolescent egotism that made us unduly conscious of ourselves and our own appearance if we're to be at ease in the presence of strangers.

Many people have developed the habit of making themselves fascinating despite physical handicaps that would drive others into retirement.

A few weeks ago I had lunch with an old friend. He's a well-known newspaper columnist. I hadn't seen him in years and we reminisced about our boyhood. It was a pleasant hour. As we reached the stairs at the exit I saw his hand grope uncertainly for the rail. Finally his fingers touched it, then his hand slid along it and guided him as he walked down confidently. If I hadn't noticed that one uncertain gesture I'd never have suspected that he was losing his sight.

"Is it bad, Jim?" I asked as we went down the stairs?

"Well, as long as I can see light and darkness, it won't be too bad," he answered. "If I lose that I'll be rather helpless."

We shook hands and separated. I knew he didn't want help. He never would have mentioned his trouble if I hadn't noticed. And it hadn't made him shy or afraid or bitter. His conversation was so alive and interesting that I didn't notice anything wrong until I saw that gesture at the rail. He must have been groping a little with his food, too. But his conversation kept me from seeing that.

I've related this incident for a very simple reason. If a man who is nearing blindness can spend an hour with a friend without mentioning his handicap, what right have we to feel shy in the presence of a stranger?

If you believe you are shy and if you want to overcome your shyness, you may want to use some or all of the following suggestions.

1. *Take care of yourself.* Grow in health and right habits. Dress well. It gives you confidence. Be neat. The slovenly man or woman knows that he is slovenly; knows also that others see his slovenliness. Stand, sit, and walk well. Act the part of a confident man or woman and you will be confident. Invest wisely in your appearance, for as someone has said, "Your presence determines your future."

2. *Speak well.* Say what you mean and mean what you say. Take some speech lessons if you need them. Get training in public speaking. Develop the art of conversation. Study the ways of the courteous listener. Remember that good speech is always two-way communication. As you talk, think of what you are saying; think also about your listeners. Look at them with a pleasant, responsive expression. You will then not have time to think about yourself.

3. *Expect interruptions.* They come in social as well as business conversation. Any business conference is likely to be broken into by phone calls. Interruptions help to make chit-chat lively. Don't let them throw you off balance. Remember the point you are interrupted at and take it up if you want to, when your turn comes again. Once you learn to do this, you will have poise. It's good for you and makes an impression of the right sort.

4. *Believe in yourself.* You are an important person. You

have many fine abilities and capacities. You are endowed richly. To prove it, make a list of all the ways in which you exceed the *average:* health, income, job, education, ideals, etc. While you may not exceed in all of them, you will be above-average in some of them. These are your blessings. In drawing up your list you will undoubtedly uncover elements in your life that you can change for the better. Change them, a step at a time. Get help if you need it. Doing all or some of these things must surely help you to grow in confidence—to believe in yourself.

5. *Think of the other fellow.* He too has problems. There are times in his life when doubt, worry, and fear loom large. He may be shy. Be sympathetic. Forget yourself in trying to see his point of view. Be a warm, compassionate human being. Shyness can't exist in your life then. Study human nature. Be humble before that great complex, the human personality. Remember, "The proper study of mankind is man." For once you get the other person's point of view, your perspective on yourself will be wholesome.

6. *Develop interests and share them.* No one knows how many hobbies Americans pursue, but one authority estimates them to be more than a million. If you believe shyness is a personal problem, develop hobbies that you can share with others. Set up a schedule so you will spend one or two nights each week meeting people of similar interests. Take courses of study at a school or college or by correspondence. You will get outside yourself that way. Life will be much more worth living. Your new interests and friends will make your personality more attractive. You will be proud of yourself. You will not have time to be shy.

If up to now you have been gripped by shyness, it will naturally take time to overcome it. You may expect an occasional setback. Your task is to break old habits, old attitudes. But remember, shyness is an ogre of your own mind. Get rid

# 8. Use These Ten Ways to Overcome Fear of Public Speaking

CAPTAIN EDDIE RICKENBACKER came home from World War I to a hero's welcome. The "ace of aces" had personally downed twenty-one German airplanes and four observation balloons in those long-ago days when planes were kites. "When I was racing an automobile," he said, "I had learned that you can't set stock in public adoration or your clippings. By the time I was twenty-six I'd heard crowds of 100,000 scream my name, but a week later they couldn't remember who I was. You're a hero today and a bum tomorrow —hero to zero I sometimes say. Never count on the crowd to take care of you."

Despite his long acquaintance with crowds, when called upon to say a few words at a great banquet in his honor at the Hotel Waldorf-Astoria, he was scared stiff. He mumbled a terrified phrase or two and sat down. That night in his hotel he actually wept for shame.

But notice the way of a winner: Next day he hired a voice coach connected with the Metropolitan Opera Company to teach him how to talk. Then he persuaded the famous newspaper writer Damon Runyon to write him a speech. He memorized it. He took up the study of grammar and vocabulary. Before long he went on a forty-night lecture tour at $1,000 a lecture. His conquest of fear of an audience has paid off handsomely ever since.

In 1926, he went to work for General Motors and became an officer of its aircraft subsidiaries. In that position he criss-crossed the country as a public speaker. The success of Eastern Airlines, which he has headed since 1938, is due in no small measure to his success as a public speaker. The only airline never to be in the red, Eastern in 1947, when other lines lost a total of $20,000,000 made $1,300,000. Always in demand as a speaker, he has made and continues to make friends for his company with these public appearances. He's at home before groups of all sizes: banquets, conventions, newspaper interviews, conferences, and the like.

Captain Eddie has a wonderful, old-fashioned American philosophy. He lives by it. One of the things he believes in with his whole might is, "Do the thing you fear." He proved the worth of that motto to him when he overcame his platform fright. It is excellent advice for the millions of men and women who are terrified to get up on their feet and speak to a group of people.

If you are afraid to speak before an audience, cheer up. You have plenty of company. Even more comforting is the fact that all successful public speakers are afraid, especially just before they begin to speak. This holds true for the most seasoned of them. It holds true also for famous actors and singers.

A few years ago John Lane wrote "Take A Deep Breath" for Collier's. He reported the results of his interviews with leading Broadway actors. He asked them if they experienced stage fright. Boris Karloff said, "I shudder and shake before every scene. After twenty-five years, too." Eva Le Gallienne had just completed her one thousandth performance when

Lane questioned her. "Yes," she said, "and it gets worse every year." Caruso, after a lifetime on the operatic stage, still maintained, "I'm scared to death each time before the first note comes out of my throat." And Otis Skinner, in his fiftieth year on the stage, described how his heart pounded and his mouth dried up just before his first entrance. Top-notchers, all of them, yet platform fright was their common lot.

How fortunate they were! For if they had been too sure of themselves, they would not have become spellbinders. The best advice to one who hopes to be a successful public speaker is, "Always be just a little afraid when you face your audience." For the speaker who is too relaxed; who takes the audience too much for granted; who doesn't tense himself for success—invariably does a poor job.

Psychologist C. W. Lomas studied groups of speakers: those who were scared to death; those who showed some apprehension; those who were overconfident. The second group made the best speeches; did the best job of moving their audiences.

Dr. Russell Potter is director of Columbia University's famed Institute of Arts and Sciences. Each year he contracts with more than a hundred well-known men and women to speak before students and others in Columbia's Macmillan Theater. He also presides at the meetings, where he is in an excellent position to study the speakers and their influence on the audience. He tells me that those who talk too easily don't hold the audience as well as those speakers who are mildly keyed up.

Seasoned speakers have to guard against becoming too casual before their audiences. "After a while," says Dr. Potter, "a speaker may become so relaxed and sure of his success that he just turns on the words and lets them flow without much conviction. When that happens the speaker needs a jolt." He needs, evidently, a bit of fear to put him on his guard against failure.

If you believe your fear of public speaking is beyond the successful amount, analyze it. Once you find the key to it you can unlock the door to platform proficiency. Here are ten questions to help you analyze your fear of public speaking.

PLATFORM FRIGHT QUESTIONNAIRE

1. *Does my fear of an audience go back to an unhappy childhood experience?* Like Bill, you may have an old, festered memory of an audience. When he was four, his mother had him recite a poem at a church sociable. He began the jingle well enough but forgot the third line. After two or three fumbles the audience tittered. That did it. He ran off the stage crying. His self-esteem and sense of security were ruined. His mother hadn't coached him thoroughly. She didn't make him overlearn the piece so he could repeat it parrotlike in a strange situation. He still suffers whenever he recalls his part in that church sociable. And like the burnt child and fire, he fears audiences.

Can Bill be re-conditioned; made into a good speaker? Of course. His first step is to change his attitude. He has to reset his sights. His first unhappy appearance before an audience took place when he was four. Now he is thirty-four. Then he had to repeat from memory. Now he may use notes; etc. In other words, Bill will do well to repeat: "When I was a child, I spake as a child. I understood as a child. I thought as a child; but when I became a man, I put away childish things."

A good way for him to put away this childish recollection is to begin to speak before audiences. At first he may wish to read an announcement at a meeting. Later on, he may read longer passages, such as the secretary's minutes. If he is wise, he will master the reading matter so that he can glance up from the paper and look at the audience.

Just as soon as his confidence is restored through reading aloud, he is ready to make motions from the floor. By gradually working on the principle of from simple to complex he will soon have no more fear of speaking before an audience than is good for him.

2. *Does my fear of an audience spring from my feeling of inadequacy in the use of the language?* Captain Eddie Rickenbacker wasn't afraid of crowds. He was frightened when called upon to speak because he was ashamed of his vocabulary and grammar; didn't have any ideas in mind; felt that his voice wouldn't carry. Just as soon as he studied and coached to make up these deficiencies he became an excellent public speaker.

3. *Am I afraid I will lose face by speaking in public?* One of the basic reasons why many of us fear audiences beyond the ordinary is that we have too little sense of humor. We take ourselves too seriously. We believe we are more important than we really are. When we get such unrealistic notions our fear is not so much of the audience, it is that we won't meet the unrealistic standards we impose upon ourselves. We feel that the audience will have a higher opinion of us if we don't speak. Now of course, if what you say is important—and if you believe in it—then you should say it. By losing yourself in your subject you won't have time to wonder "How am I doing?" In that way you really rise and shine.

4. *Is my dread of an audience a neurotic symptom?* Everyone is neurotic to an extent. Some of our quirks attach themselves to speaking situations. Professor Elwood Murray, of the University of Denver, gave the *Bernreuter Personality Inventory* to twenty-five superior speakers and twenty-five poor speakers. He found that the excellent speakers' scores were high on self-sufficiency, dominance, extroversion. The poor speakers got low scores on those three important traits of personality.

If, after due study, you feel the cause of your great fear (of public speaking) is a serious neurosis, then of course you will be wise to seek out a psychologist or psychiatrist. He will be able to help you, so that you can learn to face an audience as well as the next fellow.

5. *Is my fear of an audience instinctive?* Dr. W. H. R. Rivers is one of a number of psychologists who believe that stage fright is instinctive. When you face a large group for the first time, your inclination is to do one of three things: (1) run away; (2) become angry; (3) collapse. You feel alone, overpowered by numbers.

If, then, you believe your fear of audiences is instinctive, don't excuse yourself from learning to be a good public speaker. Your knowledge of what causes you to feel as you do is in itself power to propel you to success. Turn your fearful feelings into anger, if you must. This will make you aggressive, sort of "fightin' mad" to succeed. You will then speak out in a strong voice. You will be alert. You will be full of vigor and action. You will make the audience sit up and take notice. Your anger—at yourself for being so afraid—plus thorough preparation, will add up to a successful performance. And as you become a seasoned public speaker, your instinctive fear will grow less. But don't let it vanish completely else you will become lackluster.

6. *Is my fear of an audience due to inexperience?* You may never have had an opportunity to speak before a group. Hearing others tell of their platform terrors may have discouraged you from giving yourself a fair chance. And so you may not know what your feelings and ability would really be like before a formal audience.

Or, you may say to yourself, "Oh, I know I would fail! After all, what a wretched conversationalist I am!" Let's suppose your powers of conversation leave much to be desired. It does not therefore follow that you will be a poor public speaker.

The human personality is a mighty inconsistent complex. I know, for example, a man who stutters everywhere except in front of a microphone. There he earns his living as an announcer. Heywood Broun, the late newspaper columnist, was an engaging conversationalist but no great shakes as a public speaker. A Presbyterian minister, a friend of mine, hesitates and misarticulates in his conversation. In the pulpit, he is a compelling orator.

Psychologists offer many explanations for these inconsistencies. But the fact for you to face is this: whatever your conversational inadequacies, you need not reveal them before an audience. For one thing, you may have little interest in the chitchat that is the lifeblood of good conversation, but rise to the task of putting across your convictions to an audience. Until you try it, how will you know what you can do? Accept, therefore, the next invitation to address an audience. When you do, hold success in your mind. And you will probably be pleasantly amazed at the results. The sound of well-earned applause will repay you handsomely for your courage and preparation.

7. *Have I unknowingly cultivated fear of audiences?* Many of us actually dread the responsibility that comes with success. A young man of twenty-four, whom I know, recently had a nervous breakdown that came on him when he refused a promotion. He was a salesman of furniture. His company wanted to promote him to a divisional managership. In that job he would have to conduct meetings with groups of salesmen. "I can't understand why I didn't accept it," he said. "I owed it to my wife and son." The conflict in his mind broke him down.

His bottom problem was an emotional immaturity that

would not permit him to face high responsibility. His excuse was that he feared failure in conducting sales conferences. Somewhere in the *Book of Job,* Job says, "That which I have feared has come upon me." A great truth. We can actually bring upon us the fears we conjure up.

One of the best weapons against this sort of thing is an overdose of humility. Humility comes to us when we realize this truth: All of us are born with capacities or gifts that we must use in constructive ways. If we don't use them wisely, we must pay a heavy fine in dissatisfaction and frustration. The young man I just referred to graduated from one of our most distinguished universities. His I.Q. is high. He has an excellent personality. Until he learned that he was simply an instrument of expression and service, he remained an emotional infant. Once he accepted that truth, he gave himself away in service. Now he uses his rich gifts. Result, he is happy in shouldering high responsibility. His fear of audiences is gone. For he knows that public speaking is simply one means to achieve worthy aims.

These seven questions, then, will help you find the cause of your fear of public speaking. Think about them. Turn them over in your mind at odd moments. Keep your thinking on a calm plane. Don't feel guilty about your fear of public speaking. Say to yourself, "I'll find the cause, alone or with help, and then I'll do something about it. For there is no insurmountable barrier to my doing a competent job of public speaking."

Here are some definite steps for you to take to become a winner as a public speaker.

SEVEN STEPS TO BECOME AN EFFECTIVE PUBLIC SPEAKER

1. *Get training.* You recognize the truth in the old psychological law: "We succeed in that which we like; we like that in which we succeed." Public speaking, like all other forms of

expression, is based on technique. You can learn the technique either on your own—through trial and error—or with the help of a teacher. The teacher provides the more economical way. He saves you time and embarrassment. He channels your fears into accomplishment. In a class you learn by doing, before a particularly sympathetic audience. All of you are in the same boat.

If possible, begin your training in a small class, twenty to twenty-two students. A group of this size—meeting, say, two hours a week for twelve or fifteen weeks—allows each members many speaking experiences. And it's large enough to provide you with a formal audience.

Choose a teacher who makes you practice rather than lectures to you. Remember, you learn better by doing than by listening to someone expound upon the theory of public speaking. The vast popularity of the Dale Carnegie course in public speaking is due, I believe, to Mr. Carnegie's insistence on practice. Many of his students are college and university graduates who have had public-speaking courses as undergraduates. Too often, these collegiate courses emphasize rhetoric and other theoretical matters to the exclusion of enough practice. Result is, when these men and women get out into the world of work they feel the need of more practical speaking instruction. And so they join the practice-type course.

Adult education programs everywhere these days offer courses in practical public speaking, voice and diction, vocabulary building, and the like. They are among the most popular. As you become interested in public speaking, you will find that you can profit from related courses of study.

The head of one of New York's produce exchanges had spoken many times before audiences. One day he asked a friend to tell him how he could improve his technique. "I'm glad you asked, and I hope you won't mind my telling you that I heard you mispronounce five or six words the last time I heard you speak in public." That was enough to convince the fellow that he needed a course in pronunciation.

As I write this, one of the nation's leading newspapers has an article about the doubts that organized labor in a Midwestern state has that its candidate for United States Senator will win. The reason? Because his public speeches are full of crudities of grammer. His opponent is a polished public speaker. In the old days, many a politician won votes by speaking in the lingo of the illiterate. But education is now so widespread that that kind of appeal is suspect. It no longer brings in votes, save possibly in the most benighted parts of the hinterland.

If you are well grounded in pronunciation, vocabulary, grammar, and voice cultivation before you get your training in public speaking, you have fewer obstacles to hop over. You have, as a matter of fact, more assurance. Because every time you have qualms about using, for instance, "lie" instead of "lay," every time you pronounce a word without being sure you are pronouncing it correctly, every time you hesitate before "between you and me"—you unnerve yourself. On the other hand, when you report to a public-speaking class with well-established speech habits, you can devote all your attention to "platform business."

2. *Put your class experience into daily use.* If you don't make use of the training you get in class, you will of course not grow in composure before audiences. Your aim will be to apply what you learn as often as you can. Do you belong to a service club, such as Rotarians, Kiwanis, Lions, Chamber of Commerce, Safety Council? Do you take an active part in the meetings of your Parent-Teacher Associations? Are you active in fraternal organizations, such as the Masons, Knights of Columbus, B'nai B'rith, Altrusa? Do you help raise funds for the Red Cross or Community Chest? By making appeals be-

fore groups? Each one of these organizations will provide you with opportunities to improve your public speaking. And at the same time they offer the opportunity to serve others. An excellent combination. As you become wrapped up in the activities and welfare of your clubs and organizations, your fund of ideas grows. Your assurance mounts. Your words carry increased conviction and persuasion. When this happens you look forward with pleasure to your public speaking experience.

3. *Always speak with enthusiasm.* Psychologists recommend to those who fear audiences "the vigorous action technique." This means that you reduce your fear and tension when you let yourself go. Use gestures. Nod your head sometimes. Shake it occasionally. Let your audience know how you feel about what you say. Emphasize the important words of your statements. Let these come out louder than the others. Speak on subjects that interest you deeply. That way you become so engrossed in your convictions you don't have time to think about fear. Move around from time to time. This helps the audience to keep its attention centered on you, and it helps you to release muscular tenseness.

4. *Use notes discreetly, if you need them.* If you feel fortified with notes, by all means use them. Arrange them on three-by-five cards to fit into your hand, or to put on the lectern. Don't write out and memorize your speech. Not only will it sound rather wooden that way, but you increase your tension. What if you should forget a word, line, or paragraph? Your whole speech would fizzle out. But a few notes spaced widely, so you can easily find what you are looking for without losing your hold on the audience, will be a comfort to you. What will probably happen is this: You will prepare your talk so well—will have the main points so clearly in mind —that you won't need to look at your notes very much. Per-

haps not at all. You will prepare them mainly to bolster your assurance.

There are a number of reasons why you won't have to refer to them often. In the first place, you will arrange your ideas logically. Then one idea naturally grows out of the one before it. You will also probably want to work out a mnemonic system, so that the ideas will be there in your memory as you need them. Another reason: when you rehearse your speech each day you won't put ideas always in the same words. You will have the ideas so well outlined that the words to express them will take care of themselves. This way of rehearsing does two things for you. It builds up your word power. It releases you from the strain of parrot-memorizing.

Perhaps the best reason why you won't want to refer to your notes too much was discovered by Psychologist H. T. Moore. Dr. Moore posed the question, "Which impresses an audience more, speaking with or without notes?" He set up an experiment. He lectured to some of his classes from notes. To other classes he spoke without notes. Then he gave them a quiz. The classes he lectured to without notes remembered 36 per cent more. You and I, as members of many an audience, can testify that speakers who talk without constantly referring to notes are impressive.

5. *Talk about subjects that interest you, those you are familiar with.* If you could turn back the calendar and ask Demosthenes or Daniel Webster to speak about Einstein's theory of relativity, they would be stumped. But if you assigned Demosthenes "Greek Philosophy" and Daniel Webster "The American Constitution," you would be rewarded with two top-notch extemporaneous speeches. For they would be browsing in their favorite pastures.

When outgrowing platform fright, you will make things easy for yourself if you talk about something interesting to you. Take a subject you know thoroughly. Examples: What you like about your job; What you would do if you could begin your education all over again; Why you vote as you do. Subjects like these lend themselves well to your first assignments in public-speaking class.

Later on, when you speak before other groups, choose a topic close to your heart and an intimate part of your knowledge. If you agree to talk about something you have only a bowing acquaintance with, do a lot of reading and research. This is the way to give yourself confidence, for you can then refer to authorities.

6. *Learn from other speakers.* Now that you are resolved to overcome your platform fear, you will use the strengths and weaknesses of other speakers to help you learn what and what not to do. You may want to carry in your mind, as you listen, a list of questions, such as:

1. Does the speaker see himself as his audience sees him? That is, is he neat? Well groomed? Is his posture good to look at?
2. Does the speaker use facial expression to help put his message across? Is he "deadpan"? Does he look scared to death? Assured? Does he use a variety of expressions?
3. Does he enunciate his words clearly? Does he slur? Does he go to the other extreme and overemphasize unimportant words?
4. Does he use standard pronunciation? Any mispronunciations? Does he give you the impression that he pronounces words as do the educated people of his community?
5. Is his voice powerful enough to make you hear without straining? Is his voice flexible? Does it break? Does he use it persuasively?
6. Is his vocabulary adequate? Pretentious or pedantic? Does he use words in a way to pique your interest and imagination?

7. Is his grammar reasonably accurate? Does he use outlandish forms, such as double negatives, illogical sequence of tenses?

8. Are his gestures helpful in communicating his ideas and appeals? Does he deliver them with assurance and conviction. Any nervous mannerisms?

9. Do his opening remarks make you sit up and pay close attention? Or does he let you down with a needless apology or some other trite way of beginning?

10. Does his speech follow a plan that is easy for you to follow? Does he wander aimlessly from topic to topic?

11. Are his concluding remarks attractive? Does he summarize? When he is finished, has he left you with a message so clearly stated that you can take it away with you?

12. Is his flow of words smooth—free from "uhs" and "ers"? Does he pause at the right places? Does he speak too slow? Too fast? Does he vary his rate of speaking to fit his ideas and emotions? Or is he monotonous?

13. Is his reasoning sound? Does he jump at conclusions? Is he too emotional in his thinking?

14. Does he use vivid examples? Enough of them to put his points across in an interesting way.

15. Is he energetic? Does he put enough enthusiasm and conviction into what he says to hold your attention?

16. Is his contact with the audience good? Does he reach all parts of the audience by shifting his gaze from time to time? Does he always speak to people rather than to chandeliers, chairs, windows, etc?

17. Is what he says worth listening to? Does he speak down to his audience? Over its head?

18. Is your total impression of him as a speaker favorable? Unfavorable?

19. What have you learned from him (or her) that will make your own next speech a better one than the last one?

7. *Keep your audience's point of view*. Put yourself in the seats of the audience. Use the "you" and "we" approach, rather than "I." Speak in short sentences. Make them easy for your listeners to understand. Use a lot of examples and stories to illustrate your points. Keep your audience amused, curious, mentally panting for your next idea.

Surely one of the greatest speakers of all time was Jesus of Nazareth. They flocked to hear him in such crowds that at times he had to speak from a fisherman's boat, offshore, to avoid the press. He held them with parables—simple stories and illustrations close to their everyday lives and common experiences. His language was beautiful because he kept it simple. He made it appeal to their imagination. And with all this disarming simplicity he taught the profoundest truths. Unless he had kept their point of view in mind, they would not have stayed to listen.

There is another meaning to this admonition: "Keep the audience's point of view." The meaning is full of comfort and good cheer for all those whose dread of public speaking has held them back. It is this: The audience's sympathy is with you. It wants you to succeed. It always does unless you antagonize it. Its heart actually goes out to the lone speaker on the platform, for it puts itself in the speaker's boots. So, if you will hold that thought: that the audience is on your side; it wants you to talk well—you will have an additional guarantee to give a good speech. It too will be a powerful antidote against the poison of stage fright.

# 9.   End the Fear of Poverty
in This Way

JUDGE NATHAN SWEEDLER of Brooklyn conducted one of the first "good-will courts," back in the thirties. He wanted to help men and women iron out their problems without suing one another. He wanted to ease the crowded court calendar. He wanted also to prevent unnecessary cases from going to law. And so, each week he would ask two or three educators, clergymen, psychologists or physicians to sit with him of an evening to hear cases informally. The advice and suggestions these experts gave the distressed often helped to solve their problem informally.

One of the cases I clearly remember involved a janitor of an apartment house. He and his wife got $75.00 a month for taking care of the building where they lived, rent free. The landlord paid their electric, water and gas bills. The janitor came to Judge Sweedler's Good Will Court because he was afraid his landlord would hear about his problem and fire him.

The problem was common enough. The janitor and his wife were in debt. They had bought an electric refrigerator, electric stove, a vacuum cleaner and secondhand car—all on the deferred payment plan. Their total installments each month came to $83.00—eight dollars more, mind you, than their total monthly income.

"How have you managed to keep your head above water up to now?" one of us asked.

"Oh, we have been spelling our payments. We let some of them wait until they threaten us with court action. We sorta make Peter wait while we pay Paul. We have to buy groceries, you know. (Why didn't you think of that before . . . ?) We never thought of cheating them. . . . We're honest; we work hard. . . . We just want more time. . . . We'll pay everything up. Please don't let them garnishee my husband's wages. Can you make them give us more time? . . . Won't you tell them not to tell the landlord on us? . . . It's awfully hard to get a job in the depression. . . ."

"Do you wish to enrich Pythocles?" said Epicurus back around 325 B.C. "Then do not add to his riches; subtract from his desires." Aren't too many of us like the child that wants to eat its cake and have it too? And aren't many of the things we want truly unimportant in the long run?

We found out, as a matter of fact, that the janitor's wife could have used the vacuum cleaner belonging to the apartment house— But no, she must have her own. A perfectly laudable wish provided she had the money to pay for it. She had always cooked on a gas stove and well enough too, according to her husband. Why, for heaven's sake, must she have an electric range? (Her sister had recently got one. . . .)

Like so many other of us Americans, the janitor and his wife let their desire for things outrun their pocketbook. Result: loads of misery and haunting fear. Does this mean we should never buy on the installment plan? Never borrow money? Probably not. Almost everyone at sometime or another has to pay for things or services on the deferred plan. As a good example, many of us own our home and reduce the mortgage every month. We pay it off like rent. This is, in the eyes of thoughtful people, an excellent way. It encourages thrift and regular savings.

Again, there are times when loans have to be made for emergencies. Someone has to have a surgical operation. Junior's tuition fees come due and he must continue his education. The point I am trying to make is that we Americans buy too many *unnecessary* things before we have the money to pay for them. We mortgage our peace of mind at too high a price. We allow fear and worry to sweep over us because we forget Mr. Micawber's rueful advice. "Annual income £20, annual expenditures 19.6, result happiness. Annual income £20, annual expenditure 20.6, result misery."

We need more old-fashioned prudence in our lives. Every time you buy something on the installment plan, you pay on a dead horse. That is, you pay interest and service fees that you could use otherwise. The way to free yourself from many an anxiety and worry about money is to wait to buy what you want until you have the money to pay for it. The good old law of $2 \times 2 = 4$ is a simple antidote for many a monetary problem, personal and governmental.

"But isn't indebtedness an incentive to a young man?" Yes, we are told it is at times. I have already pointed out how a mortgage on a home, suited to your income, may be a wonderful investment. But why not forgo that mink coat, or high-powered car, or a larger diamond ring until you can really afford it? You will get more for your money that way. You will sleep better of nights. So, don't get into hot water as the janitor and his wife did. Resolve your money worries by sticking to simple arithmetic. Be content with what your income will buy. Don't try to keep up with the Joneses on borrowed money.

In December of 1732, Benjamin Franklin, then twenty-six years old and a rising young Philadelphia printer, published the first number of his *Poor Richard's Almanak*. Today Poor Richard is remembered as a model of thrift, industry and independence. Each year Franklin wrote a long preface for his almanac, and in 1757, when the taxes caused by the French and Indian War were bearing down on the colonists, he wrote to show that the taxes could be paid easily if the people would be a little less extravagant. He wrote the preface a quarter of a century after the first almanac, and it was his final contribution to the magazine.

Already he was a wealthy and famous man, after much early struggle and self-denial. Nine years before, he had retired from active business. The final preface was published on the eve of his departure for England, where he was to be the agent from Pennsylvania for the next five years.

The preface takes the form of a speech at an auction where an old man, Father Abraham, on being asked what he thinks of the times, rises and says:

> Friends and neighbors, the taxes are indeed very heavy, and if those laid on by the government were the only ones we had to pay, we might more easily discharge them; but we have many others, and much more grievous to some of us. We are taxed twice as much by our idleness, three times as much by our own pride, and four times as much by our folly, and from these taxes the commissioners cannot ease or deliver us by allowing an abatement.

Today as we face enormous taxation as in Franklin's time, we also have the personal liabilities of idleness, pride, and folly. And it would be well for us to reread Ben's wonderful prefaces. For if all of us would follow his sage advice our money worries would take pretty good care of themselves.

Did you know that of all things husbands and wives fight over, money heads the list? Sociologists have studied divorce proceedings and found this to be true. This fact leads some to conclude that money differences is the chief cause of divorce. We also know the divorce rate is no higher among the low-income groups than among the high-income groups. It isn't the size of the income that determines happiness in marriage, it is the regularity of the income, the way it is spent, and the attitudes of those who spend it that really count.

Most of the young couples that come to us with money worries don't live on a budget. Usually they have never talked over a spending plan before they married. Take John and Mary ——. Mary was an only child whose father allowed her rather free use of charge accounts in department stores. He was wealthy and indulged his charming daughter's taste for expensive clothes. She fell in love with John, an accountant, and married him after an engagement of about six months.

Four or five months after they came back from their honeymoon they were quarreling bitterly about money. John hit the ceiling when the bills from the stores came in, and Mary felt hurt that he didn't see eye to eye with her father. Yet they loved each other enough to work out a plan. First and foremost: no more charge accounts. Fortunately, John advanced fast so that he provided for Mary quite well. Today she is eager to discourage brides from getting the charge-account habit, because she knows that it almost wrecked her marriage.

Until a young married couple lay down the rules of the financial game they must play together their marriage will be spoiled by needless bickering. Like a pack of ten-year-olds on a baseball diamond, they will spend too much time fighting about the rules. In the old days before so many women went out to work— (Remember, one out of every three married women now helps to support the family.) —the breadwinner could make *his* rules stick.

If he was a curmudgeon and would give you only $x$ dollars a week for the table; and if you had to say "pretty please" every time you needed a box of handkerchiefs—you might grumble. But you could actually do little else. Eventually you learned to grin and bear it or work out forms of genteel blackmail to bring him to heel. For those were the days when you couldn't very well go to work and of course you never thought of getting a divorce. What would the neighbors say? A divorced woman simply had no standing.

Today the windmill turns in the other direction. If you are a stingy and selfish husband, your wife can tell you to go to blazes. She can get a job and earn as much—sometimes more —than you. If she likes you on other counts, she may let you stay married to her. If not, there's always Reno assuring her a warm welcome. The neighbors? Well, they don't swing as much weight as they used to.

Of course the most successful marriages are based on rules made in a spirit of compromise by both partners. Rules about spending, love-making, child rearing, hobbies, relatives, common interests, religion, and the like. The best way for most of us to state the rules about spending money is to draw up and follow a budget.

When the word *budget* first came into use in the English language in 1432, it meant a bag or wallet. Not until fairly recently did it mean a financial statement or spending plan. Is it a cure-all for money worries? No, but it helps a lot. And the best time for most couples to begin to build a budget is *before* they marry. Talking together about their future in hard cash terms helps to make the marriage a success. For if the two of you swallow only bowls of sunshine during the courtship and honeymoon, you will, I can promise you, gnash your teeth after you marry.

Given: a couple with a steady income; the knowledge how to build a budget; the character to keep within it. Result: most of their monetary woes float out to sea and sink. So, if you would rid your life of money worries or fear of poverty

—especially if you are married—build and follow a budget. Of course a good budget for Tom and Mary may not be satisfactory for Tim and Madge. Even so, certain well-known basic principles of spending money can help the Toms and Marys, the Tims and Madges, work out their way to freedom from financial worries.

TEN RULES FOR COUPLES TO SPEND MONEY WISELY

1. *Form a partnership*. Decide that your first basic principle is to share and share alike. After deciding what part of the income is to be spent for living expenses and what is to be saved in the form of insurance, savings bank account, etc., divide whatever is left into two equal parts. One-half of this belongs to Mary; the other half to John. If Mary wants to spend her share of the "leftover money" on a collection of charms for her bracelet, all right. If John wants to put all of his spending money in tools for his workbench, all right. No matter how small the amount may be for pocket money, let it be "equal shares for each." No strings attached. You see, this permits each of you some financial independence, a little freewheeling, as it were, for your own cherished interest.

2. *Spend less than you earn*. Always keep within your income. In the beginning of your married life together there will be many temptations to spend everything you make. Your attitude might easily be, "We're young only once. We're not making much now, anyhow. We want to entertain our friends a lot. We'll wait to save when our income is larger." No, set the habit at once. If your income is very modest, your savings in the beginning may not be more than a few coins a week dropped into a piggy bank. But at least you're getting off on the right foot.

3. *Put your savings to work*. You will not keep your savings under the mattress. Don't let them sleep. Keep them working.

After you have taken out your life insurance policy, you will probably next build up a savings account where your money will draw interest. Choose a bank that compounds the interest, semiannually, or, better still, quarterly. Someone asked Thomas Alva Edison once who the greatest inventor of all time was. The Wizard of Menlo Park answered that one in a hurry: "The fellow who invented compound interest."

All your wishes to be financially independent, to have more nice things in your life, can be realized through savings. Nothing will prove the power of your sustained effort as well as the fact that a dime doubled twenty times becomes $209,715.20! The interest that your money draws compounded, hurries along the day to realize your great expectations.

After your savings account is big enough to take care of the usual emergencies, you may want to consider buying a few shares of stocks, blue-chip variety of course. Bought at the right time, they pay excellent dividends and provide growth of your principal. If you had invested $2,750 in 100 shares of International Business Machines common stock in 1914 and held on to it, and exercised all subsequent purchase rights costing you $6,364, by now your holdings would be worth $546,992 and you would also have received $153,404 in dividends! Our other great companies, such as General Electric, Standard Oil of New Jersey, and I. E. DuPont de Nemours Company, are similar miracles of growth. You will of course always put your savings to work under the best advice you can get. In every community, banks have officials who can put you in the way of the best kind of investment information.

4. *Build Your Budget on Percentages.* You may want to buy an excellent book, such as *How To Make Your Budget Balance* by E. C. Harwood and Helen Fowle, published by The American Institute for Economic Research, 54 Dunster Street,

Cambridge, Massachusetts. It is paper bound, contains 143 pages, and costs only $1.00. Here you can get detailed guidance for apportioning your income wisely.

If you don't want to work on a detailed budget, you will find the general principle of percentages a good one to follow. For example, in New York City where rent is notoriously high, you may spend 25 per cent or more of your income for your apartment. In most parts of the country, the budget authorities advise the average head of a family to spend no more than 20 per cent of his wages on rent. If you decide to own your own home, you will be safe if you buy one that costs no more than 300 per cent of your annual salary.

You may be puzzled as to how to begin allocating your income according to the percentage plan. Why not be guided by the experience of about 4,000 families whose budgets were recently studied by experts? All of them had moderate incomes. They spent about 40 per cent of their total income for food; 15 per cent for rent; 16 per cent for clothing; 12 per cent for household operation, and 17 percent for miscellaneous items.

When you think in terms of percentages you have a handy measuring stick to hold your enthusiasms in check. You face realities that way. You are not so likely to go off the deep end and buy an eight-cylinder car instead of the four-cylinder job that suits your income better. Budget percentages help you to think clearly about the ways in which you plan to spend your money.

5. *Plan your purchases ahead.* I pity a young couple whose parents provide them with everything in the way of worldly goods at the beginning of their marriage. Such a couple miss a great deal. They never know the thrill of studying catalogues and advertisements together. They are strangers to the art of window shopping. They are deprived of the delicious experience of making a choice: say, between an arm-

chair or a new set of china. They don't know what it is to
grow together in the exciting task of building up a home.
They must be strong indeed of character and good will to
make their marriage survive without this cementing process.

For successful marriages are based on a working partnership, each partner taking an active part in the planning and
carrying-through of the total responsibilities. The reason why
the divorce rate is so much lower among the rural than city
population of our country lies here. For the farmer and his
wife work together throughout the day in winning a living
from their land. They plan together; they eat together three
times a day. Whereas in the city, husbands and wives are separated so much of the time. They live independent lives.
They don't work together enough. Too many of their interests are away from the hearth.

Another reason why you should plan purchases well ahead
is to discourage *impulse buying*. Did you know that all our
great merchandisers employ experts to study the chinks in
your armor? They rig up mass displays. They put attractive
merchandise within your actual reach. You take it up and
fondle it. It becomes a part of you. You can't put it back.
You often find when you get home that you bought it when
you didn't mean to; when you didn't actually need it. Be
smart. Don't let them influence you against your better judgment. Draw up a list of things you need. Then buy those.
Check them off as you buy them. Don't become an *impulse
buyer*.

6. *Keep a record of what you actually spend.* This helps you
improve your budgeting. Just now inflation faces Tim and
Madge. Although their income has increased, prices have out-
distanced it. Their income tax has gone up too. Their real
income, therefore, has shrunk. They have to cut down. And
so they turn to last year's record of what they spent. Instead
of guessing or calling on vagrant memory, they see right off

the wasteful or unnecessary items. Tim and Madge buy a ledger at the corner store—one will last for many years. They keep it simply and list such items as those shown on the chart facing this page.

You can, of course, make your budget much more detailed, but Tim and Madge's covers the main items. At the end of the year their record helps them when they prepare their income tax return. It also puts their home on an efficient, businesslike basis. Don't you see how their ledger helps them avoid needless bickering?

Marcia is on a reducing diet. She tells me she is encouraged to stay on her diet because the mark she makes on the graph each morning repays her for her loss of luscious calories. "It's fun, you know. But not nearly so much fun as Russell and I have keeping our accounts together. We keep Monday evening, right after dinner, for casting up our accounts." Why not something similar?

7. *Deny yourself.* It's good for your character. Can you afford to smoke a pack and a half of cigarettes every day? Multiply the cost by 365. Why not cut down to a half pack? Why not stop smoking? Right after World War II, George —— came to see whether we could help him get a job. He had just given up his college course under the GI Bill of Rights.

"Why give up your wonderful chance to get a college education on Uncle Sam?"

"Oh, I can't live on the allotment. You see, I was an officer in the Air Corps. I earned a lot of money and got expensive tastes."

"Why not drop some of your expensive tastes? For example, I notice you smoke cigars. Why not a pipe?"

"Oh, cigars mean an awful lot to me. . . ."

George, George, what a foolish fellow you are! Always think of first things first. "Whatever necessity lays upon thee, endure," the great Goethe would say to you. "Whatever she

| | Jan. | Feb. | Mar. | Apr. | May | June | July | Aug. | Sept. | Oct. | Nov. | Dec. |
|---|---|---|---|---|---|---|---|---|---|---|---|---|
| Food | | | | | | | | | | | | |
| Rent | | | | | | | | | | | | |
| Insurance | | | | | | | | | | | | |
| Taxes | | | | | | | | | | | | |
|   income | | | | | | | | | | | | |
|   property | | | | | | | | | | | | |
|   sales | | | | | | | | | | | | |
| Transportation | | | | | | | | | | | | |
| Fuel | | | | | | | | | | | | |
| Household expenses | | | | | | | | | | | | |
|   electricity | | | | | | | | | | | | |
|   gas | | | | | | | | | | | | |
|   water | | | | | | | | | | | | |
|   soap | | | | | | | | | | | | |
| Medical care | | | | | | | | | | | | |
| Dental care | | | | | | | | | | | | |
| Savings | | | | | | | | | | | | |
| Recreation | | | | | | | | | | | | |
| Clothes | | | | | | | | | | | | |
| Contributions | | | | | | | | | | | | |
| Newspapers and magazines | | | | | | | | | | | | |
| Gifts | | | | | | | | | | | | |
| Old age pension | | | | | | | | | | | | |

commands, do." Deny yourself. Make sacrifices, especially for those that are real investments. Get your education and you can smoke much better cigars in the long run.

Tim and Madge, you are wise when you deny yourself that automobile so you can have a home of your own. Save. Budget. Do with less in order that you may have more eventually. The automobile will come in time. But your home will do more for your marriage in the meantime.

8. *Limit the sum you carry with you.* If you have been careless about money, train yourself to respect it. Learn the value of a dollar. Limit yourself to so much a day. Then take only that much with you, and make it do. Know what you have in your purse. If you are like Marjorie, you carry your whole allowance with you. By Wednesday, it's almost gone. And then you borrow from your friends. No, you'll never be free from money worries if you don't change your ways, Marjorie. You will make a poor risk as a wife. You will not be a good example for your youngsters. Be prudent. Change your money ways.

Gus was a goodhearted fellow who married in his late thirties. He earned $75.00 a week driving a truck. After he gave Jennie $40.00 to "run the house" he put the rest in his wallet. What happened to it? Well, he played the pin-ball machines. He was always good for a touch. People seldom paid him back. He liked to treat the boys to a beer. By the week end he had nothing to show. Jennie grew resentful. Their youngster's prospects for a college education are dim. And Gus, believe it or not, has little respect coming from his "friends." Behind his back they actually make fun of him. Deny yourself, Gus, it's later than you think. Get wise.

9. *Be a wise bargain hunter.* One of the wholesome developments in our schools within recent years is the subject usually called *practical home economics.* Many young wives

are doing magnificent jobs as buyers for their families because in school they learned the technique of getting their money's worth. They know how to get a lot for their dollar. They are a walking *Prudence Penny*. One of the principles they had drummed into them, "Don't buy simply because it's cheap," is top advice.

If your education didn't include such a course, you can still learn to buy wisely. You and your husband may want to take a course in home management together in a night school. You and he can study recommendations made by consumer-associations. Ask your public librarian for books and pamphlets on the subject. You can also learn to be a better buyer by trial and error. Patronize those stores and outlets that maintain a fine reputation for honorable dealing. Take advantage of bona fide sales. Jot down in your memo book which stores have sales when—and what their specialties are. Remember, a penny saved is a penny earned. I am forever amazed at the happy faculty many young wives develop for prudent buying. Anyone with an eye can hold a dollar bill to the light and see the colored silk in it. But only wise buyers can see the rubber in it as well. For the dollar bill does have stretching qualities—in the right hands.

10. *Buy quality.* Mollie and Jane are two pretty stenographers. Both of them earn $45.00 a week. Both are single. Mollie has twice as many clothes as Jane. But Jane's dresses, suits, and hats are better looking. They are in excellent taste—quiet and chic. They fit better, wear longer. Jane looks like a million dollars, but Mollie's clothes are on the shoddy side. Jane of course buys quality; Mollie buys quantity. Both spend the same sum for clothing. Which does a better job of buying?

In the last ten years Sam has bought three lawn mowers, each of them a cheap piece of merchandise. His neighbor,

Albert, bought one for the total cost of Sam's three. Albert's mower is twelve years old and still going strong. Which bought quality?

If you are observant you have noticed that some families of modest means collect useful objects of beauty over the years. Others, in the same income brackets, have nothing but "junk." You can be sure the first family is a buyer of quality and the second isn't. The point I'm trying to make is that quality in the long run is cheaper and better. By using our wits, we can have many of the good things of life at no greater cost than the other kind.

Here again we see how using our common sense can solve our money worries and a basic fear—the fear of poverty.

# 10. Say Good-by to the Fear of Old Age

THE HOT AIR CLUB, an aging but happy clan of theater folk, recently celebrated the half-century of its existence, on Long Island. The members held their annual clambake—a traditional feast of clams and clam chowder, lobster and buttered corn, French fried potatoes and apple pie. Members of the club belong to the business side of the theater. They are all more than sixty years old, many of them in their seventies and eighties. As press agents, theater managers, box office treasurers, and producers, they are too busy leading the strenuous life to fear old age.

For most of them, their annual reunion is their only opportunity to see old friends and to recall the parade of the theater since they first knew it. Their club hasn't changed through the years. It holds no business meetings, has no bylaws, collects no dues. One of its octogenarian members, an ex-producer, says "The club has existed for half a century on sentiment alone."

Sentiment has apparently done an excellent job of keeping them young and active. For they are without exception an optimistic, jolly lot. They began their club purely by chance. In July, 1898, some of them were talking business at the bar of the old Fifth Avenue Hotel. And one of those present had just returned from a clambake. Pleased with its bounty and good fellowship, he suggested that the group treat themselves to a similar feast.

"That's a lot of hot air!" said one of the men at the bar, and by unanimous agreement the organization had a name. They held the first clambake the following July, and the club's first president received a bottle of air (undoubtedly hot). Ever since, the incoming president is presented with a similar token of esteem along with quips and jokes from each member.

The menu of the Hot Air Club remains the same. The members' names—living and gone—are printed on it, under the club's creed:

> He that eateth well, drinketh well;
> He that drinketh well, sleepeth well;
> He that sleepeth well, sinneth not;
> And he that sinneth not goeth straight
> Through Purgatory to Paradise.

One of the members, a booking agent for most of his life, said at a recent meeting, "There's nothing like the club. We come together just to shake each other's hand, just to be with one another. And we keep going in the profession which we love so dearly—well—just so long as we can manage to navigate. It's our world and it means the world to us."

What the world needs obviously is many more clubs like the Hot Air Club. We need to wage war on the fear of old age, that fear which is uppermost in millions of lives today. A hundred years ago only 1 out of every 38 Americans was over 65 years old. By 1900 the ratio had risen to 1 out of every 25. Today the total is 1 out of every 13.

According to the minutes of the National Conference of Aging, sponsored by the Federal Security Agency, which met in August, 1950, at Washington, D.C.—the number of persons 65 years old or over had almost quadrupled in the past fifty years; from 3,080,000 in 1900 to 11,514,000 in 1950. By 1980 the country may expect to have about 2,000,000 citizens more than 65 years old.

Three miracles are responsible for our growing life spans. Medicine may take the honors for all three miracles. The old-time infant mortality rate, which was huge, has been chopped down. Cures for chronic ailments have been discovered. Many virulent diseases, such as yellow fever, diphtheria, smallpox—formerly undertakers' delights—have been virtually wiped out.

These boons of medicine, along with our widespread knowledge of good dietary and health habits, add up to a greater life expectancy for all of us. Scientists now believe that the natural human life span extends to somewhere between 115 and 125 years. The Equitable Life Assurance Society of the United States, one of America's largest insurance companies, has just recently upped its life expectancy tables to 120 years! Actuaries, who have a way of being uncannily right in such matters, tell us that in the near future the centenarian will no longer be a newsworthy item. Rather, he will be just an average specimen of normal healthy existence.

And so, the time has come to say "So-long to old age." Geriatricians, those scientists who specialize in the study of the aging process, leave us little ground for begging off from the responsibilities and joys of a busy and happy life beyond three score years. For aging, they tell us, sets in shortly after birth. That is, parts of us are on the decline from the word go. All of us are relatively young or effective in certain respects even when the years mount, particularly if we maintain a wholesome attitude. The point is to make use of our changing powers as the seasons come and go.

We must, therefore, stop linking many years with uselessness. Know that every age has its reason for being. If you will hold on to this thought, you can say good-by to your fear of old age. Consider a few worthies who thumbed their noses at Father Time. Benjamin Franklin worked diligently on a perennial best seller, his autobiography, when he was eighty, after coming home from his long, distinguished ambassadorship to France. Goethe completed what is judged by many to be the greatest single work of literature, *Faust*, when he was eighty-two. William E. Gladstone was managing the affairs of an expanding British Empire as Prime Minister at eighty-three. The creator of the Czechoslovakian Republic, Thomas G. Masaryk, was still the grand and vigorous leader of his country at eighty-seven. Clara Barton established the American National Association for First Aid when she was eighty-four. She learned to typewrite at eighty-nine.

That favorite painter of many a discriminating art lover, Titian, created some of his best masterpieces after he reached eighty. He was still going strong at ninety when the plague carried him off. Galileo discovered the diurnal and monthly changes of the moon when he was seventy-three. Verdi composed *Otello* at seventy-four and his unforgettable "Te Deum" at eighty-five. The late Commodore Vanderbilt earned well over $100,000,000 after he was seventy by increasing the mileage on his railroads from 12 miles to 10,000 miles.

Notice how the world in crisis always turns to leaders of many birthdays when great wisdom is needed. Clemenceau came out of retirement to save France in World War I when he was over eighty. England turned to Winston Churchill in her hour of greatest stress in World War II. Still the leader of his party at more than seventy-seven, he is going strong.

Look about you and you will find in every community of the land, men and women who have lived many years and remain hearty and productive. They refuse to be cowed by threescore and ten or any other pat definition of old age.

They ward off decline by keeping on their toes. And the curious thing about these stalwart oaks is that they seldom lead lives of quietude and sedateness. Rather, they weather storms of worry, frustration, excitement, and even prolonged strain in furthering their goals. Often, they are our best scouts on the front line of the human struggle.

Of course we do not look for home-run records to be broken by baseball players of fifty or seventy-five. Nor do we bet on a prize-fighter forty years old. All of which goes to show that each age has its work to do. In other words, the capacities and forces within us wax and wane, some finding their greatest fulfillment at one age, and others at another. The idea is to squeeze the most out of each passing year. In this way we keep too busy to fear old age.

That is just what Bernard M. Baruch does. (Mr. Baruch, counselor to all the Presidents of the United States from Woodrow Wilson on, is celebrating his eightieth birthday this year.) Here is his formula for staying young. I quote from an interview Mr. Baruch gave to Burnet Hershey of *The New York Times Magazine*:

1. *Don't let yourself get in a rut.* "They mentioned rest to me after World War I. I was fifty then. Supposed to be middle life, fifty is, but it's just plain youth. Didn't have time to think about rest. Sounded too much like a rut, anyway. Ruts are hazardous to intellectual keenness, and they're death on quick perception and youngness of body."

2. *Break the Rules.* "It's a habit of mine to break habits. I like to make the area of contact with all phases of life as large as possible; to spread out in many directions, mentally, sympathetically, and to penetrate deeply into some, or at least in one. I have no rules, except belief in the unswerving regularity of irregularity. I gave up smoking when I was sixty-four—simply because it didn't agree with me any more. I take a cold bath every morning. I've cut down on my drinking—and

today take very little except an occasional toast or congratulatory highball—because it doesn't agree with me.

"But there just aren't any rules. That's because old age is not inevitable. Although what we call the year period, that is the years' succession, may be advanced, old age is a state of mind that often happens to the middle-aged and some times to the old."

3. *Sleep on your problems.* He agrees with Ocar Wilde who said, "No civilized man should go to bed the same day he arises." Mr. Baruch says, "Generally I'm a late stayer-upper, but sometimes I go to bed early just to start coping with the problem of going to sleep. If you've a problem you might as well face it. And going to sleep is mine."

4. *Eat a lot.* "I'm always hungry. I eat like a young boy. Certainly I've been on diets—but that was when I had the gout. A man should learn self-control. I never have."

5. *Pace yourself.* "Men often don't pace themselves well. They drive too hard toward breakdowns, toward the wear and tear of their tissues, and then, suddenly, they drop. Mind you, again, there's no rule, not even here. Some men might do their best this way. But the idea of frequent short vacations is a good one. Only if it suits—never if it doesn't."

6. *Do what you like doing.* "I go down to my farm in South Carolina, mostly in winter, from Thanksgiving to the first of March. There I'll go shooting wild birds up to the limit that the law will allow. You know, I can still sit in the saddle for from two to four hours and follow the dogs. But that's because I like it—not because I think it's healthy. The minute I stop liking it, I'll stop it."

7. *Believe in free enterprise.* "A man who is free can mold his life, just as a nation that is free can mold its life—even control, to an extent, the building forces of his body and brain just as we can today control great forces of nature in electronics, dynamics and atomic energy."

8. *Help solve the problems of the aged.* "As I see it there are two issues to be faced. First, we must throw out our depression-born philosophy of forcing older workers out of jobs just because they are old. Broadly speaking, it is unwise to judge a man by his years—when his faculties are as keen as those of younger men. And second, we must check all forms of inflation, because if we don't our plans for old-age benefits, private annuities and even savings, will be useless when the time comes to use them."

Don't you see how a philosophy like Mr. Baruch's is in itself insurance against decrepitude? I like particularly his insistence that it is unwise to judge a man by his years when his faculties are as keen as those of youngsters. Right here let me emphasize that there is too much misinformation about old age. Too many of us associate gray hair with ineptitude. Those of us who do are way off base. The fallacy is being disproved at every turn.

Dr. Ross Armstrong McFarland, of Harvard Medical School, reveals in a recent report that "oldsters" are more stable than the average young worker. They do not tend to be afflicted with that malaise of the green years, sometimes referred to as *antis pantis* or *termitis trouserus*. Dr. McFarland also reports that the oldsters change their jobs less often and have far fewer accidents. One study concludes with this interesting finding: mill hands over sixty years of age have only half as many accidents as those in their early twenties. We also know from the records of automobile accidents that men and women drivers between fifty and sixty are safer drivers than the youngsters.

Age-old prejudice seems to be responsible for the widespread erroneous belief that older workers are too slow and inflexible. The fact that they make up in skill and endurance what they lose in strength and quickness is overlooked on all sides. Remember the years of World War II? How the old-sters turned in a magnificent record of production? Heart-warming examples, like the widow of General Longstreet—famous Civil War Confederate Leader—were common oc-currences. Near the fourscore mark, Mrs. Longstreet enlisted in a training course, completed it, and did her stint in an air-plane factory.

Or take the vocation of civil air pilots as a stiff example. Under high-altitude flying conditions, where the oxygen pres-sure is reduced, those of more advanced years actually do better than their young colleagues. They are less liable to fainting and collapse because their cardiovascular systems are more stable, and they suffer less loss of memory. Many authorities now believe that pilots sixty years old can pass tough tests of flying vision. One large transcontinental avia-tion company has one hundred pilots over forty years of age! So, the postwar world of an autogyro in every garage, or should we say, hangar, need hold no terror for those who have voted these many years.

To be sure, psychologists have known for a long time that by fifty years of age most men and women have lost some sen-sory acuteness. As a matter of fact, our senses work at their highest efficiency during the second decade of life. At that time we taste more lustily, hear more sharply, see more acutely, have finer control of our muscular co-ordinations than during any other decade.

But still, individuals vary greatly in these matters. One recent study showed that of a group of men and women work-ers in their fifties, 25 per cent had better vision than the aver-age man in his twenties. Many people forget that inventions and scientific discoveries provide compensation for the flag-ging senses: spectacles and hearing aids, for example, when properly fitted, can keep an individual eternally young in re-gard to sight and hearing; vitamins and hormones are also boons. The Fountain of Youth is under our very noses, if we will only look for it.

Nature provides a compensation for the early decline of our physical forces by increasing our mental abilities with the advancing years. On the average, mental maturity is not reached until forty, and even continues to increase slowly until sixty. With exercises, our mental powers are practically as good at eighty as at thirty-five. Please remember we are talking about averages, and that state of health, inherited predisposition, and environment may alter the outlook for the individual.

We age unevenly; not as a unit. The thymus gland, for instance, ordinarily atrophies by three years of age, before the child has grown into ways of logic. Wasn't it Havelock Ellis, in his *Man and Woman,* who reported that our heads continue to grow until we reach the middle forties? Some of our organs and capacities may grow old prematurely while others retain their vitality up to the greatest longevity. In short, our chronological age as measured in years does not always coincide with our physiological age or psychological age as measured by the functions of the body and mind respectively. The secret of being able to say "So-long to old age" is self-study and the early selection of exercises and compensations to thwart the gremlins of vigor.

The problem is world-wide. Sir William Beveridge's famous report to the English Parliament, *Social Insurance & Allied Services,* contains some interesting figures: in 1931, the percentage of the total population under fifteen in England was 24.2, while the population of men over sixty-five and women over sixty was 9.6 per cent. In 1971, there will be 16.5 in the youth group and 20.8 in the old-age group. The world is marching toward maturity.

In one of his speeches Cicero declaimed, "Intelligence and reflection and judgment reside in old men, and if there had been none of them no state could exist at all." What with the increase of maturity throughout the world we may expect the creation of happier and more seasoned governments because the state is the sum of its citizens. If, then, our older citizens continue active and make the most of their powers with the advancing years, we can anticipate a better world.

Why? Because people who have lived a long time are more seasoned. They take things with a grain of salt. They are more tolerant of the frailties that man is heir to—more understanding, if you please. The human relations of men and women of advanced years are invariably superior to those of an equal number of youngsters. Using his judgment, accumulated experience, and mental training, the person of years can apply his wisdom which youth's inexperience doesn't permit. It takes most of us about fifty years really to plumb our limitations and abilities. Socrates, who preached *Know Thyself* to youth, was preparing them for the leadership of later life.

Once we have learned what we can and cannot do through trial and error (or success) we have a realistic basis on which to succeed in living the good life. Someone observed that "A new and strengthened purpose, unhampered by emotions and ambitions, can often accomplish tasks that were inhibited by the impatience and resistance of younger years." Purposive living never grows old or decrepit.

That brings us to an important question all of us must face sooner or later. "How can I rid myself of the fear of growing old?" The question is a good one to ask ourselves shortly after we're old enough to vote. For the best time to wave good-by to superannuation is long before it actually begins.

1. *Develop interests and more interests.* The late Carr V. Van Anda, the famous managing editor of *The New York Times,* retired at the summit of a distinguished career "to gain a larger leisure for the intellectual life." From then

until he reached seventy-nine he made himself an authority in mathematics and astronomy.

Judge Robert W. Winston of North Carolina, retired from the practice of law to improve his golf. He found this wasn't enough to keep him occupied. So he entered the University of North Carolina as a freshman at the age of sixty. After his college course he wrote substantial biographies of Andrew Johnson, Jefferson Davis, and Robert E. Lee. When he was seventy-seven he published his autobiography, *It's A Far Cry*.

Henry Wadsworth Longfellow addressed his classmates at Bowdoin College when they celebrated their fiftieth reunion. He recited a poem he wrote for the occasion:

> Cato learned Greek at eighty, Sophocles
> Wrote his grand Oedipus, and Simonides
> Bore off the prize of verse from his compeers
> When each had numbered more than four score years.
> Goethe at Weimar, toiling to the last,
> Completed *Faust* when eighty years were past
> Chaucer at Woodstock, with the nightingales,
> At sixty wrote *The Canterbury Tales*.

He of course pointed out that they were exceptions, but he also emphasized that many more of us can do excellent work in the golden years. "They go to show," he said, "how far the Gulf Stream of our youth may flow into the Arctic current of our lives."

At the Hudson Memorial Center in New York City, hundreds of retired men and women flock to classes in all sorts of subjects to meet their interests. Have you found out what courses are open to you in your community? At the Hayden Planetarium, the Amateur Astronomers Association sponsors a course popular among the oldsters—Telescope Making. They grind their own lenses and fit them into a tube so that they may study the stars at home.

You, perhaps, know of many subjects you would like to explore. If so, why not become an inveterate reader? Your local library will help you lay out a long-range reading program. With a little thought and discussion you can unearth a thousand and one things to do with your time. Perhaps, like "Grandma" Moses, who took up painting after she passed seventy, you will find a new world of interest in canvas and paint brushes.

You will find that the more interests you develop, the greater your mental alertness will be. Interests keep you so preoccupied, you don't have time to long for the "good old days." You will find the days of the present even better. Avid interests help digestion, dispel insomnia, make tomorrow a happy anticipation. Hobbies of all kinds make excellent interests. Learning new things—a foreign language, say—is tops. Remember that the psychologists have proved that the adage "You can't teach an old dog new tricks" is absolutely wrong.

2. *Cement old friendships, make many new friends.* Do you know about the Three-Quarter Century Clubs? Mrs. Evelyn Barton Rittenhouse, a former actress, founded the first chapter in St. Petersburg, Florida, for retired men and women at least seventy-five years old. Now, you will find Three-Quarter Century Clubs in Iowa, Maine, Michigan, and Vermont. Miami, New York, Norfolk, Richmond, and Providence have Threescore and Ten Clubs. You will find Borrowed Time Clubs in cities like Lima, Ohio, and Oak Park, Illinois.

The members of these clubs have a good time doing things together. They play shuffleboard, golf, and tennis. They organize and attend dances. They even have soft-ball teams. Several years after Mrs. Rittenhouse formed her club, its soft-ball team named itself the Kids & Kubs. The players averaged almost eighty years of age. One time an eighty-four-year-old missed making a home run because he stopped to pick up something between third and home base. When his teammates bawled him out, he snapped, "Well, doggone it, I dropped my teeth."

On the same team was a retired minister. One day he collided with another player and they started an argument. When the minister recalled his vocation he said, "Brother, I'm sorry. Forgive me. There for a minute I forgot I was a minister and not a baseball player."

Some of the members are old enough to have children in the club. Andrew Stodel celebrated his 100th birthday in the club by going swimming. His daughter, Mrs. Hanna Ulman, belongs to the same club as her father.

A few years ago the club sponsored a boxing championship for the "Whiskerweight" title. George Washington Brown, weighing in at ninety-two years, and Corporal Williams Chubb, aged ninety, were the contenders. The referee was Charles Eldridge, one hundred and four.

For those who like less strenuous activities, there's the "Mighty Ninety Quartet," composed of men over ninety. The oldest member is ninety-seven. They are directed twice a week in their rehearsals by John B. Shirley, more than seventy-five.

All these activities result in friendships. Here you associate with those of similar problems and interests. You are in a sympathetic climate. You discover that old age has a charm and happiness all its own. At times you may even feel sorry for youth's greenness. You pride yourself on the deeper insight that has come to you with the passing of the years. And you find that old age holds no insurmountable fears. And so you resolve to build up your friendships immediately.

3. *Marry again.* My former colleague, Tom, retired from his professorship at sixty-five to move to California with his wife. They had been married thirty-five years. She died unexpectedly shortly after they got out there. And he was

unconsolable. "Why?" he would write hsi friends. "Why did this have to happen after we had laid such happy plans for our last years together?" He allowed it to prey on his mind, and within a year he followed her into the great hereafter.

I have another friend of about the same age as Tom was who also lost his wife recently. Let's call him Jake. So far as I can tell, Jake loved his wife as dearly as Tom loved his. But Jake resolved to take another view. "For some reason beyond my comprehension," he said, "I have been left behind to carry on. Our marriage was a good one. Martha would want me to have companionship just as I would want her not to be lonely." And so, after two years, Jake looked for another wife. He made a wise choice, for he and his new wife (a widow) are resolved to make each other happy.

And what better time of life to share sorrows and joys with a mate in marriage? For the vast majority of men and women, marriage provides them with the best way of life. The later years together are often the sweetest. Remember Browning's famous lines?

> Grow old along with me!
> The best is yet to be,
> The last of life, for which the first was made.

The idea is to stave off loneliness, that incubator of fear. And one of the best ways to do this, if you are a widow or widower, is to marry again. Remember, those who have already had one successful marriage have the wisdom to make another succeed.

4. *Take reasonably good care of your health.* Get your physical check-up regularly. Study your body's changing needs as Bernard Baruch tells us he does. Andrew —— at sixty-five finds that his digestion improved when he gave up

smoking. His wife had just the opposite experience. She began to smoke at sixty years and lays her improved digestion to her after-meal cigarette. A woman I used to know recently died in her ninetieth year. She drank ten cups of coffee a day as long as her family could remember. Until shortly before her death, she stayed healthy and alert. Through intelligent self-study and little experimenting we can, each of us, discover the best regimen for us.

A danger we face these days is standardization. The holy average is held up to us as the ideal to follow. They tell us how many hours we ought to sleep; what room temperature to work in; what to eat and what not to eat; and so on. Yet no two people, according to careful research, react to the same stimulus in exactly the same way. Their needs vary a lot. One man stays in the pink of condition at seventy years without taking any exercise. His twin sister must walk two miles a day to stay healthy.

Averages, you know, may actually be dangerous to live by. Remember the fellow who drowned in the stream whose average depth was only two feet? The best one to say what is best for you in these matters of health, is *you*—if you take the time for intelligent self-study, along with due consideration of what your doctor recommends. The point is, the healthier you keep yourself, the easier it is to prevent the fear of old age. For what we most fear about the advanced years is not age itself so much as the infirmities that so often go with it when we don't take care of ourselves.

Every day new medical discoveries are adding to the health of the older patient. A few years ago, if you were threescore years and ten, the best treatment you could expect from a physician was a word of encouragement and a reminder that he didn't have a remedy for old age. If you suffered from a malignant growth, nobody would touch you. You were a poor surgical risk. In the old days, if you were disturbed by a depression or neurosis or arthritis, treatment was considered hopeless because of your advanced years.

Now this attitude has changed entirely. If you are an older patient you are ordinarily considered an excellent surgical risk. Every day the chronic ailments of later life become more and more amenable to treatment. An old person of the middle of the twentieth century is no longer necessarily a sick person. He is a human being with a future. That means, investment in his health and social status will result in productive returns.

5. *Keep in mind the financial adjustments you will have to make.* If you have to move to smaller living quarters make that move in the years when you still receive your full income. Plan for your retirement not later than eight or ten years before you reach retirement age, preferably much earlier. Make sure that you receive all the benefits you are entitled to. We are, as a nation, making increased payments to help the retired. This year, 1952, old-age benefits amount to more than $3,000,000,000. Back in 1939, the figure was much smaller, only $601,000,000. In 1960, the estimated total benefits to be paid 14,700,000 men and women expected to be over sixty-five, if held to the present payments, will add up to $6,767,000,000. If the allotment per person at retirement were to be stepped up to $100.00 a month, as it may well be, $17,600,000 would be paid out.

In order to make your dollars stretch, you may decide to move from an expensive locality, such as a large city to a small town. Some of the southern states provide many more comforts for reduced income than others.

One other suggestion that seems to be tremenduously important: Don't hesitate to accept help from your children. Remember the days of your bounty and generosity. Time and again we receive appeals from children at the National

Institute for Human Relations to persuade their parents to accept money from their child. They are too proud. They forget that a stern and sometimes necessary test of character is to receive rather than to give. Ask yourself, "If the tables were turned, wouldn't I do the same?"

6. *Take a part-time job.* Particularly, if you are the kind of person who doesn't know how to occupy his spare time. Some of us are so constituted that, to be happy, we need a regular schedule to follow. Even though we may have enough money to live on, we take secret pride in bringing home a weekly pay check when most of our friends are in retirement. If a job means so much to you, you will either get one through the usual channels, or make one for yourself.

In Denmark, the Titan Machine Company, one of the largest industries in the country, has recently opened a factory employing only workers over sixty-five. It has a four-hour day. We need factories like this in the U.S.

Hundreds of jobs are open to those of the advanced years. Here are just a few examples. Proxy Parents is a New York agency that supplies baby-sitters. Only women, more than fifty years of age, are employed. Once on the Proxy Parents list, they may work a few or many hours a week, as they prefer. This organization, and others like it, have learned from experience that the older woman makes the most reliable and useful baby-sitter.

Many a retired policeman, finding time heavy on his hands, gets a job as a night watchman. One of the largest banks in New York, having more than fifty branches, makes it a practice of hiring retired policemen as daytime guards.

Several grandmothers I know deliver telegrams. They like to be out of doors. They enjoy meeting people. Some of them drive their own car. Others work routes in the business districts where not much walking is necessary. Not one of these women in my acquaintance has to work. One of them has a right to be proud of herself because she uses the money she earns to help send a grandson through medical college. The vocational guidance agencies in your community can help you find jobs open to you.

I said earlier that you may wish to make a job for yourself. One good way to do this is to start a business. Perhaps your neighborhood needs a baby-sitter agency. More babies are being born in America these days than ever before. And more mothers are going out to work. Baby-sitters, therefore, have a bright present and future.

I met a woman recently, between sixty-five and seventy, who a year or two ago began a service that is paying off very well. She sold executives in the midtown area of New York City on the idea of letting her maintain bouquets in their reception rooms. Every day, she or an assistant replaces wilted flowers with fresh ones. She told me she could expand her business if she wished to, but she wants no more responsibility than she already has created for herself.

A man of sixty-three lost his savings two or three years ago through speculation. He tried, unsuccessfully, to get a job as bookkeeper, his former vocation. Then he hit on the idea of selling box lunches. He now has a thriving business, delivering coffee and sandwiches to office workers. His company will deliver your breakfast, lunch, or dinner. He tells me he is now planning to branch out, catering to birthday and holiday parties held in offices and factories.

Another retired man I know in New Jersey organized a housekeeping service. He will arrange to wash your windows, clean one or more of your rooms, mow your lawn, etc. You may hire his company's services by the hour, day, or week. Right after the war, he hired only ex-GI's and featured that fact in his advertising.

Well, you see there are ways and means of making a job

for yourself, if you want one. None of those I have mentioned were expensive to start; all of them were easy to sell because they offered needed services. Undoubtedly there are such needs, and others, in your own neighborhood.

7. *Go back to school.* Dr. Martin Gumpert in his book, *You Are Younger Than You Think,* says that education for longer life should have four goals: (1) The preservation of our social functions requiring a continuity throughout our whole life span, of growth, information, knowlege and understanding; (2) The preservation of health; (3) The preservation of skill; (4) The preservation of our emotions and inspirations.

You will be pleasantly amazed, if you have not already made inquiries, how many opportunities exist in your community for you to go back to school. Adult education is moving along at a tremendous momentum. You can meet the objectives expressed so well by Dr. Gumpert by going back to school. Get in touch with your local Board of Education. If it shouldn't have a course to meet your interests, it will help you find a correspondence course, perhaps sponsored by your state's Department of Education. You will keep so busy that way, you won't have time to pamper your fears.

One of the chief reasons why you will enjoy going back to school is the new friends you will make. The course you take will attract the right sort. Some men and women are touched with inspiration. We like to be with them because they stimulate us in the right way. These people are good for us and should be cultivated throughout life. Dr. John H. Finley, after spending a lifetime as professor and education administrator, managed one of the country's leading newspapers as its editor, after he passed seventy. He used to say that his formula for staying young was simple: "Every day take a long walk, read a good book, and make a new friend." When you go back to school you can take a walk, read a good book, and make many new friends.

8. *Keep your sense of humor.* They tell the story of William R. Jackson, the famous photographer for whom Jackson Hole, Wyoming, is named, if I remember correctly. Jackson had his photograph taken on his ninety-eighth birthday. The photographer was a cheerful fellow who said after he'd finished, "Thank you, Mr. Jackson, I sure hope I'll be round to take your picture when you're a hundred."

Jackson gave him a twinkle and answered, "Why not? You look pretty healthy."

When the great jurist Oliver Wendell Holmes was past ninety, he and a friend were taking a walk in Washington, and an attractive young woman passed them at a merry clip. Holmes sighed to his friend, "Oh, to be seventy again."

Of course, keeping your sense of humor means much more than the ability to throw out a good quip now and then. It means keeping your problems in perspective, not taking them —and especially yourself—too seriously. As you look back upon the crises in your life, you realize as you grow older that they took rather good care of themselves. They always did better, as a matter of fact, when you kept calm and busy. During World War I, David Lloyd George carried the burdens of leadership of the British Empire. Yet he stayed pink and fresh. When asked how he did it, he replied, "Make the most of troubles. As far as I am concerned, a change of troubles is as good as a vacation."

I am convinced that men and women of many years are either very popular or very unpopular with young folks. The popular ones are they who have kept their sense of humor.

During World War II, when General Douglas MacArthur was in the Philippines, he kept above his desk on the wall this choice passage, based on a poem by Samuel Ullman:

Youth is not a time of life—it is a state of mind; it is a temper of the will, a quality of the imagination, a vigor of the emotions, a predominance of courage over timidity, of the appetite for adventure over love of ease.

Nobody grows old merely by living a number of years; people grow old only by deserting their ideals. Years wrinkle the skin, but to give up enthusiasm wrinkles the soul. Worry, doubt, self-distrust, fear and despair—these are the long, long years that bow the head and turn the growing spirit back to dust.

Whether seventy or sixteen, there is in every being's heart the love of wonder, the sweet amazement at the stars and the starlike things and thoughts, the undaunted challenge of events, the unfailing childlike appetite for what next, and the joy and game of life.

You are as young as your faith, as old as your doubt; as young as your self-confidence, as old as your fear; as young as your hope, as old as your despair.

So long as your heart receives messages of beauty, cheer, courage, grandeur and power from the earth, from man and from the Infinite, so long you are young.

When the wires are all down and all the central place of your heart is covered with the snows of pessimism and the ice of cynicism, then you are grown old indeed and may God have mercy on your soul.

# 11.  Rear Your Children to Be Fearless

DURING WORLD WAR II, many of our brave boys in the South Pacific (and elsewhere) had nervous breakdowns. But the army psychiatrists were amazed out there by the calmness of the savages. Driven from their homes by the enemy, their way of life turned topsy-turvy, their loved ones mutilated and killed before their eyes—the savages did not break down.

"How can this be?" said the doctors of the mind. "Our boys who crack up have had rich advantages such as the natives never even dreamed of. They are well educated. They are provided with good food, clothing, entertainment, and so forth. They get regular physical check-ups; medication whenever they need it. Yet the underprivileged aborigines bear their hardships like stoics."

After careful study, the psychiatrists came to the conclusion that these savages were unusually tender and loving parents, even as their mothers and fathers before them. As a baby you were carried on your mother's back until you walked. You always felt the warm security of her body, so long as you were an infant. She petted you a lot. She fed you at the breast whenever you wanted it. She did not let you cry.

Her primordial wisdom told her she must keep you happy. That crying is a sign of pain. That happy babies don't cry without cause. Your mother always had time for you and your wants. From the first day of your life she dedicated herself to providing you with a happy childhood. And she didn't delegate your care to someone else. From the beginning you were an important part of her life, of your family's life.

The result was, you grew up with a deep sense of emotional security. In your mother you had a love-object you knew would never let you down. You belonged. When you outgrew infancy, the whole tribe helped to make you feel wanted. For they respect children as individuals. You could always count on being loved. You played and shared with other children. You were so strong in happy memories, you could face the devil himself without breaking down. From birth your environment disposed you to happiness. Your happy attitude was so deeply rooted, it carried you over the rough spots of later life. Anxiety and fear and hardship could not make a nervous wreck of you.

On the other hand, the psychiatrists discovered that our psychoneurotic boys had repressed fears extending back to their early childhood. They heard about them when they put the boys under *narcosynthesis*. That is, they administered a barbiturate drug to them—sodium penitol or sodium amytal —until they became sleepy. Under this condition the patient relived the battle experience that brought on the breakdown. With the psychiatrist's help the boy was able to recall the painful childhood memories that produced his symptoms. With each treatment he released his pent-up fears and hatreds. His psychiatrist acted as a substitute for his family and lead him back to wholesome attitudes. When that happened the boy was cured!

You see, therefore, that we must provide our youngsters with love and understanding. Otherwise the steady rise in nervous breakdowns, the soaring divorce rate, and all sorts of delinquency, crime, alcoholism, suicide, and job dissatisfaction will continue to increase. For you can trace the cause of most of these tragedies to an unhappy, insecure early childhood.

Did you know, for example, that divorce is inherited? Not biologically of course. But children of divorced parents have a significantly high divorce rate. Take three large groups of couples married ten or fifteen years ago. Goup A is made up of wives and husbands who were reared in happy homes. In Group B, one spouse of each couple comes from a broken home. In Group C, all the men and women had parents who divorced or separated. Now trace divorce among the three groups, and you will find an interesting fact. Group C has ten times the divorces of Group A; Group B, six times the number. Do you see how we conclude that divorce is inherited?

The authorities tell us that poverty isn't the main cause of crime and delinquency. Young delinquents come from all economic levels. The constant factor is the lack of enough love and understanding in their early lives. They become fearful and do things that society doesn't approve of. That's another reason why we need to understand youngsters better; to love them more tenderly.

As babies, all our actions are directed toward satisfying bodily wants. We unknowingly seek pleasure and comfort. That is, a powerful drive in all of us at birth is the *id*. We have it in common with the animals. For example, in the first few weeks we sleep almost all the time except when hunger pains wake us. Our sleep is deep, restful, carefree. Obviously, we enjoy it. Just as soon as we feel hunger pains, we wake up and cry. Once fed, we feel comfortable again and go back to sleep. We can't get enough pleasurable feelings.

Our insistence on pleasant feelings stays with us throughout life, although we learn to harness it when necessary. The most civilized host in the world may feel hungry at the sight of a steak, but instead of grabbing it, he politely carves it and serves each one of his guests before he begins to eat. When you hear adults say that the end of life is comfort, many of them mean "satisfying the id." As one philosopher puts it, "The sole motive of every action of man is the desire for happiness."

But let's return to baby. He is around two years old when he first realizes that "I" is different from "You." At that time he enters the stage of the *ego*. Now is the time he puts "I," "me," and "mine" in most of his expressions. You might say his motto is "Where do I come in?" He is a selfish fellow. He thinks very little about the comfort of others.

All selfishness that you and I meet, wherever we live or work, springs from the id and ego. For example, I have never known a divorced couple, either of whom or both did not suffer from too much ego. They are childlike in this respect.

Take Gloria—beautiful and accomplished. She married a young lawyer who adored her, for the first year. After that her insistence on always having her own way got irksome. She saw that she was losing him, so she decided to have a baby. That might hold him! When the baby came she would not nurse it, although the formula didn't agree with it for a long time. "It's not going to ruin my bust-line," was all she said. When the summer came, she hired a nurse to tend the baby and spent three months at the summer cottage. In all that time she saw the baby once every two weeks. Unnatural, you say? Yes, indeed, she had ego sickness. Moreover, she was fear-ridden.

I have come to the conclusion that egocentric men and women have many more fears than the usual. They are insecure emotionally. They fear loss of face. They are strangers to the greatest of virtues, humility.

Psychologists say that the greatest single factor making for good human relations and happiness in individual life is a strong drive to express oneself in a way that will make living more pleasant for someone else. If you have such a drive, and it is strong within you, you have an outgoing, warm, unselfish personality. You are an uplift to your community, because you ease many a tension among its inhabitants. You also have the social intelligence to see that the world in which you live needs your enlightened help and good thoughts to improve it. Whenever, for example, you unselfishly help a hospital raise funds to meet its deficit; serve on a P.T.A. committee; organize a Boy Scout, Junior Achievement, or 4-H Club; lift up a weary soul—you reflect a strong *super-ego*.

Usually, the man or woman with a mature super-ego has surmounted reverses, terrors and fears, hard knocks, stiff competition, and occasional defeat. Such experiences make the ego-sick man or woman resentful, envious, and sour on life. But when you turn these hardships into understanding and sympathy, you have the insight that goes with super-ego. Others will seek you out for encouragement, for your unconquerable spirit will sparkle. It will serve as an example of fortitude. Your super-ego will thus inspire others. It will be a source of serenity to you. Hugh Walpole wrote in his novel *Fortitude*: "It isn't life that matters, 'Tis the courage you bring to it." He's right as rain.

Even the stoutest heart needs occasional encouragement. And even though reassurance may not be a cure-all for fears, it helps to lighten their dread weight. It gives a respite, a chance for you to take a deep breath and start anew. And so I say, each one of us who wishes to grow bigger of heart, deeper of understanding, must not neglect to encourage those who suffer from fear and anxiety. They need our sympathy and help.

To come back to childhood. Virtually all children have

fears. Dr. Arthur Jersild and his associates at Teachers College, Columbia University, have been studying children's fears for many years. In one study, they found only 19 youngsters out of 400, between five and twelve years of age, who said they didn't have any fears.

Dr. Jersild reports that three-year-olds admit an average of 5.5 fears. At four years of age the average number increases to 6.3 fears. Then there seems to be a decline in their fifth and sixth years to an average of 4.4 and 3.2 fears respectively. They fear all sorts of things. Many of them seem ridiculous to grownups. It is not always easy for an adult to sympathize with a moppet who fears a butterfly. But some youngsters at two or three years of age actually do fear butterflies. Of course, derision isn't an intelligent way to help the youngster overcome his fears.

Intelligent mothers and fathers help their little ones develop skills so that they will be able to cope with feared things and situations. Johnny became afraid of the dark after he was awakened one night by a loud clap of thunder. He cried and fumbled for the lamp button, but couldn't manage to light the lamp. His mother reassured him. Next day she had a pull-cord with a large tassel at the end put on the lamp. She taught Johnny how easy it was to light the lamp with the new gadget. She encouraged him to put on the light whenever he awakened. Just as soon as he realized he could have light whenever he wanted it, the dark no longer held any terror for him.

Mary, three years old, was afraid to descend the stairs after she fell headlong and hurt herself. Her mother taught her how to descend them backwards on her knees as she held on to the balustrade. After that, Mary's fear of falling down the stairs disappeared, and she soon walked down them in the usual way.

Ever since Billy was knocked down by a playful dog he was

afraid of all dogs. His mother took him to the Bronx Zoo. Quite casually, she showed him the dingo or wild dog of Australia. For the first time Billy had no fear because he saw the dingo safely behind bars. She bought Billy illustrated dog stories; and read to him heroic deeds of dogs. Finally she bought him a six-week-old puppy, so small and helpless that Billy felt masterful beside it. Before long his old fear of dogs had gone down the lane. By gradually bringing him in contact with dogs, she had solved the problem. She was a good practical psychologist.

Dr. Myrtle McGraw proved that we can rear fearless *or* fearful youngsters, whichever we choose. She took twins, Johnny and Jimmy. She was present at their birth and supervised their education from then on. Johnny was the first born; Jimmy came sixteen and a half minutes later. Both of them were of the same blood type—Group B. They looked alike. From the time they were twenty days old they were brought to Dr. McGraw's clinic five days a week. They stayed there seven hours a day. They spent all their early childhood with her and her assistants. During each day of the early months "Johnny was stimulated at two-hour intervals in order to evoke those activities which were within his scope at the time." As he grew older his exercise program became more extensive.

On the other hand, Jimmy's stimulation was definitely limited.

Dr. McGraw conducted many experiments with the twins.

Johnny was encouraged in every way possible. Jimmy was allowed like Topsy just to grow. One illustration will show how a child can be trained to be fearless. When Johnny was 395 days old he was put on a pedestal sixty-three and a quarter inches high. He would throw his body forward into the outstretched arms of Dr. McGraw or her assistant. He had been trained gradually to be accustomed to heights. After a few days he would hop from one foot to another, eagerly anticipating the jumps.

When Jimmy was 473 days he was first put on a stool for jumping into the arms of Dr. McGraw. "Although he was quite happy before, he now began crying and clinging tenaciously to the experimenter." Never once did he make the slightest move to throw himself off the stool. Later on when put on the pedestal he cried and clung to it until fatigue forced him to drop to the floor.

Which are you rearing—a Johnny or a Jimmy?

Little children because of their tiny size, dependency, and helplessness need a lot of encouragement to surmount their fears and misgivings. Robert Louis Stevenson saw the problem when he wrote,

> "The world is so big, and I am so small
> I don't think I like it at all, at all."

They need much praise, particularly when they do and try to do admirable things. They ought to be spared the endless nagging that is their common lot. For nagging is a hostile act, a sign of frustration. It makes the youngster jittery. It makes him liable to more fears than he would have otherwise. When you encourage a child (or an adult for that matter), you do not of course create strength within its breast. You merely free energies and attitudes already there. Your spark of encouragement sets the tinder of courage on fire.

Remember also that your own attitudes are contagious. When Wordsworth declared that "the child is father to the man" he had in mind the intuition that is particularly keen in little children. Even though Buddy's mother reared him "by the book," he felt a lack of affection. She saw to it that he was well clothed, properly nourished, and so on. But one day, shortly after his fourth birthday, he said to her in deep wisdom, "Mommie, you really don't love me, do you?" And he was right.

Your child knows when you are harassed, fearful, or serene, even if you don't say anything. He is a student of muscle tensions, eye expressions, voice qualities, postures, etc. If, therefore, you are a happy, courageous person, you are an excellent example to your youngster. That is the best kind of encouragement you can give him.

Alexandre Dumas, the younger, author of *Camille,* once exclaimed, "How does it happen that while children are so intelligent, men are so stupid? Education must be responsible for it." Until very recently we have done little or nothing in the schools to teach youngsters to triumph over fear. But in the public schools of Delaware, the classroom teachers are holding discussions with their youngsters about their fears and other personal problems. Dr. H. Edmund Bullis is the Director of the project.

Howard Whitman has described the project in an article in *Woman's Home Companion,* "Teach Our Children to Live." He visited a class of sixth-graders. They were having a lesson on *Our Unpleasant Emotions.* One girl explained that previously they had learned that "Our intellect deals with what we *know.* Our emotions have to do with what we *feel.* Most of the other school classes concentrate on *knowing.* This class deals with *feeling.*"

The teacher told a story about a soldier who had gone AWOL in North Africa. He had failed to understand the emotion of fear.

"Fear is certainly an unpleasant emotion," the teacher said. "What are some other unpleasant ones?"

The youngsters volunteered a dozen to put on the blackboard: hatred, anger, worry, sorrow, rage, envy, jealousy, gloom, inferiority, greediness, anxiety, shame.

"How do some of these affect us?"

Joanne answered, "One time I thought I had lost a schoolbook. I was afraid you were going to bawl me out. I worried about it and I couldn't sleep that night." "Just for the record, how did the incident turn out?"

"Well, I hadn't lost the book at all. I was frightened and I worried all for nothing."

Miss Virginia Mason, the teacher, didn't have to moralize the lesson that most of the things we worry about never happen.

Dick said, "When I'm afraid I get so weak in the legs I can hardly stand up."

Johnny had had an experience of falling off a running horse on his cousin's farm.

Before long even the shyest members of the class were talking out their pent-up feelings.

"All these are perfectly natural and normal emotions. We don't have to be afraid of them. We all have them," Miss Mason said. Then she returned to the story of the soldier, and asked, "Is there anybody who has never been afraid?"

Only one boy raised his hand. "Well, you're lucky," she remarked. "No, maybe you're not, because fear can be our friend."

The youngsters quickly took up the suggestion. Jeanne told how being frightened in a roller coaster made her hold on tighter; how even the perspiration on her hands helped her to grip the safety bars more securely. Donald told how his fear of a Great Dane kept him from being bitten by him. Rudy told how he swam faster when he saw a snake in the water.

Such examples gave Miss Mason an opportunity to separate real from foolish fears. She said that the former protect us while the latter make us ineffective.

Dick raised his hand: "When I was a little kid I was scared to go up to the attic."

"How did you overcome it?" Miss Mason inquired.

"I just went up in the attic one time. There weren't any ghosts, so I wasn't scared any more."

Miss Mason brought the discussion to a close. She said, "We should remember that we are often afraid of something because we really don't understand it. We must try always to look at it squarely. We must learn to live with fear, to use it up as we go along—not let it pile up within ourselves."

Let us hope that soon all the school systems in the country will offer instruction in how to overcome our common fears. That should go a long way to rid us of many of our repressions. A repression to me means a piling-up of fears. In repression we thrust our fears back into the subconscious mind where they fester. Often they account for the mental breakdowns in later life. And so, the sooner we resolve our fears, the better off we are. Many congratulations to Dr. H. Edmund Bullis and Miss Emily E. O'Malley of the Delaware school system for their pioneer work, *Human Relations in the Classroom,* the syllabus for the teachers in the state, to help their pupils understand and conquer their fears!

## TWELVE WAYS TO REAR A FEARLESS CHILD

Our main job as mothers and fathers is to set our children in the way they should go before the school years. Of the many ways successful parents rear their youngsters to be fearless, twelve stand in high prominence.

1. *Let the child be born into, and thrive on, an atmosphere of love.* If you are a pregnant mother, hold constantly in mind all the tender thoughts you can muster about your unborn child. "I want the baby very much. I want to nurse him and care for him. I want him to be strong and healthy. I know I shall rear him to be gentle and fearless because my love

will guide me rightly; will inspire him to be a superior individual.

Thoughts of this stripe build up the right maternal attitude. According to those who believe in the prenatal influences, such thoughts leave their wholesome impress on the unborn child. If, for some unhappy reason, you may not want the child or fear its birth, get help. For such negative thinking is hard on you; is unfair to your child; may give you extra labor pains.

During your pregnancy, share your plans and ideals with your husband. Inspire him to join you in your loving and tender thoughts. Encourage him to be an understanding husband and father. Make him proud to be the father of your child. And his love for you will deepen.

After the baby is born, nurse him at the breast, if at all possible. Some gynecologists say that as many as nine out of every ten mothers can nurse their baby, if they really want to. Actually only one out of every three in certain localities does. Breast feeding is the baby's natural right.

To the question, "What was the most tender scene you witnessed after your wife and baby came home from the hospital?" ninety-eight young husbands out of one hundred whose wives breast fed the baby, said, "Watching her suckle the baby." The other two said, "Bathing the baby." The way you tend your baby can be an inspiration to your husband as well as determine baby's early (and later) attitudes. Through word and action, let love prevail.

If you are an expectant father, be solicitous of your wife's health and spirits. Buoy her up. Make grand plans for her and the baby's future. Tell her how much you love her; how grateful you are she is bearing your child. Reassure her constantly of your devotion; prove it by your actions. Make her time easy and memorably happy. You owe it to her and your

child and to yourself. Let her pregnancy be a time of tenderness and understanding on your part. Help love crowd fear
out of your home.

2. *Make positive suggestions.* Remember, your child develops his basic attitudes toward life in his tender years. You
are responsible for his outlook. When he falls down and
hurts himself, don't say, "Poor dear, how it must hurt!" For
you make him sorry for himself that way. Say rather, "Oh,
it doesn't hurt now. Get up. You're all right, aren't you?"
Smile and encourage him to laugh. Teach him to laugh at his
minor tragedies. Help him to see the funny side of his experiences. Whenever he comes to you in good faith, take time to
compliment him. Praise him a lot, when he deserves it. Suggest to him always ideas of health, happiness, affection.

Don't let him overhear you criticize others or say unkind
things about people. Never tell him that you are afraid. Let
your positive suggestion be reflected not only in your words
but in your actions, facial expression, and deeds as well. If he
should come to you and tell you that he is afraid, suggest to
him that he need not be afraid; that you are at his side to help
him solve the fear.

Remember that when you analyze a fear of your own, you
take away many of its pangs. Help your youngster to analyze
his fears. When you do, you practice what the psychologists
call *depreciation by analysis.* The more information you provide about the feared object, the easier it is to understand. It
doesn't seem so formidable that way.

Always prepare him well in advance of his first visit to the
dentist. Select a physician or dentist who knows how to gain
the confidence of your child. Distract his attention when he
gets there. Always approach a problem with your child in
a casual, calm, unhurried way. Accent the positive elements;
deprecate the negative aspects or ignore them.

3. *Always reach your child's level of understanding.* Study

the developmental ages of childhood. You can get many excellent books from the library to help you understand the psychology of infancy; of the questioning age (from 3 to 6); of the "Big Injun" age (from 6 to 10), of the awkward age (from 10 to 16) ; of later adolescence (16 to maturity). Always realize that each age is beset with typical fears; also typical levels of understanding. Two very common fears of adolescents, for example, concern God and sex. During the awkward age, shyness and feelings of inferiority loom large. Night terrors often beset the "Big Injun" age; and so on. Don't underestimate his doubts and fears. Talk in his terms. Reach him at his level of understanding.

4. *Don't laugh at your child when he is afraid.* See his problem through his eyes. A boy of three was afraid of the shadows cast on the side of the house by a ten-year-old pear tree. He said the shadows looked like a bogey man. His mother carried him around the yard. When she got to the pear tree she moved a branch and showed him how its shadow changed. Then she and he together moved the branch. Finally, he moved it by himself. By that time he was laughing, because he had control over the shadows. And she joined in the fun. She laughed *with* him at the right time. But that is quite different from laughing *at* his fears. This intelligent mother used this advantage to talk with him about the bogey man. Where had he heard it? From some playmates. Now she had the opportunity to dispel another foolish fear.

Your most powerful weapon on fear, your own or your child's, is speech. Talk it out. Share it. Many a man and woman would be far happier if they would talk out their fears. So many of them admit to the psychologist that they never got into the habit of talking out their fears in their childhood because "the grownups laughed at our fears."

5. *Don't quarrel.* Do quarreling parents make their children fearful? Yes, says Dr. Harington V. Ingham in *The*

*American Journal of Psychiatry.* He studied two groups of students at the University of California. One group was psychoneurotic; the other, of robust mental health. As youngsters the psychoneurotic group grew up in homes where their mothers and fathers quarreled; the second group were reared in peaceful homes. Dr. Ingham comes to the conclusion that family quarrels are one of the chief causes of mental illnesses. Even the loss of a parent doesn't do as much harm to the young child's emotions. He also found that parents who stay together "for the children's sake" and can't stop quarreling, do not help their youngsters resolve their fears and doubts.

Nagging, or what I call the "no-no neurosis," is almost as bad as quarreling. Several years ago I spent a week end with some friends, and while I was apparently wrapped up in the Sunday paper I really kept count of the number of times the mother of the house said No to her three young boys. I counted as "no" such phrases as—"don't do that," "what did mama say?," "stop it or I'll have to spank," "go away." "H-e-n-r-y!" Altogether it came to 102 "noes" in a little more than sixty minutes.

At the end of that time I decided to go up to the guestroom where I could really read. Then I said "No!" I thought too much of these nice people. In fact, I decided to stick my neck out and talk to the young mother.

"Henrietta, you know, you are nagging at your boys too much. I've been keeping tabs on you. I've actually counted up one hundred and two times that you've said No to them in the last hour." Henrietta gave me an angry look. But after struggling between apathy and anger, she adopted a middle course and with a forced smile said, "All right, I'll listen. You tell me: what do I do?"

I told her: In the future, stop and think before you say No. Say to yourself, "Is this important? If it isn't really important, let it pass. That's easier said than done, but remember, unnecessary "noes" hurt your child and hurt you. They hurt you because they lessen respect for your commands.

Unnecessary "noes" hurt your boys. They confuse them because you say No indiscriminately. They love you deeply. And every time they hear you say no they feel your disapproval. Often, they feel guilty and frustrated. Such children often grow up with the "no-no-neurosis." You make them negative and stubborn. They are unhappy and may be inhibited as adults. They reach maturity with too many tensions, doubts and fears.

Many an "unnecessary no" is merely a sign of your own nervousness or high tension . . . don't take it out on your children. When you do say No say it gently but firmly and stick to it. Keep your mind on your No until you are sure your instructions have been followed. The youngsters will learn that No *means No* and their obedience becomes automatic. I remember a mother who reprimanded her daughter for disobedience and received the reply— "But you didn't insist, Mommie." When you take a stand, "insist!"

Henrietta found that life became much easier for her and the children. They quieted down. The younger boy lost his shyness with strangers. The older one ceased wetting the bed. They willingly obeyed when she cut down the number of "noes" and let them have their own way on minor waywardness even though it "got her goat" in the beginning. Her husband finds her a more gentle wife. And we are all better friends than ever.

6. *Teach your child to solve personal problems.* J. P. McEvoy tells how a friend of his learned a valuable lesson. As a boy, his mother one day called him to the kitchen, spooned a hot potato out of the kettle, and said, "Here, Son—catch!" and tossed him the hot potato. He hopped around yelling and throwing it from one hand to the other. All the while his

mother laughed and said, "You don't know what to do with it, do you?"

"But suddenly I did," said McEvoy's friend. "I threw it back at my mother, who looked surprised but caught it, dropped it in the kettle and said: 'That is something for you to remember all your life. When anybody throws you a hot potato—throw it back.' "

Later on she explained that a Hot Potato was a situation that was hard to handle. It may be a difficult question to answer. It usually comes without warning. She told him how all his life he would be meeting smart fellows who played dumb, who didn't answer questions but returned them to you. In that way they learned, she continued, what *you* know. They would study how *you* would react to the question. They wanted to see what *you* would do with the Hot Potato—to learn how *they* could handle it or to let it cool off a bit so it wouldn't burn them. Although this was a Spartan way to teach a lesson, it stuck. And the fellow profited richly from it throughout his life.

Anything you can do to develop resourcefulness in your child to solve his own problems is an excellent way to prepare him to resolve his fears and worries. For a main difference between a chronically fearful person and a courageous one is brought out in the way they handle Hot Potatoes.

The other day a neighbor of mine discovered that his seven-year-old daughter had taken some candy bars from a store without paying for them. He asked her if she thought she had done right. When she admitted her misdemeanor, he told her he could punish her in several different ways. He could spank her. Send her to bed early. Make her apologize to the storekeeper and return the candy bars, etc. He asked her which she thought was the worst punishment. She said going back to the storekeeper and admitting her theft. This he made her do. It was a wise course to take. For the girl had to do something herself about straightening out the mess she had gotten herself into.

Too often mothers and fathers give their youngsters virtually no opportunity to make decisions. They guide every step. They don't do this: "Here, Johnny, is your first allowance. You may spend it all today. If you do, you won't have anything for tomorrow or the other days, until a week from today. If you spend it all on candy and eat the candy all at once, you probably will get sick. You can, on the other hand, spend a part of it each day. It will probably be more fun that way. But it is yours. You have to make the decision how to spend it. The only thing I insist on is that once you spend it as you decide to do, don't complain. Think first before you act."

This sort of an approach teaches the youngster that freedom of decision entails responsibility. How he solves his problem of spending his first allowance—or whatever else it may be—determines in some part how he will solve his future problems. You will be an excellent parent indeed if you encourage him to solve as many of his own problems, according to his ability, as possible.

7. *Be just.* Lord Byron, the romantic and handsome poet, was an unhappy man because of his unfortunate childhood. One of the chief reasons for his unhappiness was the way his mother treated him when he was little. Herself a neurotic woman, she would smother him with hugs and kisses one minute, and throw a pair of scissors at him the next. Poor Byron had no consistent standard of conduct to measure his actions by. He was often punished when he deserved reward; and the other way around.

Mothers and fathers usually debate: To spank or not to spank? Here is a questionnaire you may wish to answer:

SPANKING QUESTIONNAIRE

Yes No 1. Do I lose my temper while spanking?

. . . . . . . . . 2. Do I feel much better after administering a spanking, as if a weight were lifted from my chest?

. . . . . . . . 3. Do I spank as hard for petty offenses as for more serious infractions?

. . . . . . . . 4. Do I experience periods when I feel the urge to spank alternating with periods when the youngster "can get away with most anything?"

. . . . . . . . 5. Does my hand feel good as I administer the spanking?

. . . . . . . . 6. Is spanking the only way I can control my children?

. . . . . . . . 7. Do I spank my children simply because my parents spanked me?

. . . . . . . . 8. Do my spouse and I have serious disagreements about spanking the children?

. . . . . . . . 9. Do things go black while I spank?

. . . . . . . . 10. Can I get as good results by using some other, gentle form of punishment?

. . . . . . . . 11. Does spanking terrify my child?

. . . . . . . . 12. Do I feel guilty after administering a spanking?

If you answer Yes to any of the questions, you probably would be well advised not to spank your children. The greatest danger in spanking is the opportunity it provides for venting deep-seated resentment. The greatest risk in not spanking is that unresourceful parents, knowing of no other way to correct their youngsters for their misdemeanors, let them grow like Topsy.

Our main problem here, as parents, is to be just when we punish. That means we must be consistent. We must be reasonable in making our standards clear to the youngsters. We must also use rewards much oftener than punishment to attain our goal. The point is that the child who is never punished is likely to be at loose ends. His fears, worries, and anxieties are often as grave as those of the overly-punished child. But the youngster reared by parents who administer rewards and punishments justly, develops a set of standards of right and wrong. These standards contribute mightily to his sense of security.

8. *Keep your child in excellent physical condition.* Dr. G. M. Stratton discovered that physical disease leaves a lasting impression on us, so that even after recovery, our resistance to fear (and anger) is permanently lowered. In other words, those of us with a history of robust health actually experience fewer fears. You see, therefore, how necessary it is to keep children in sound health. When you ward off sickness in their lives, you actually free them from fears in their later life. This means that you will help them establish in themselves regular habits of sleep, eating, elimination, cleanliness, and exercise when they are very young. Prevent disease and you prevent fear!

Youngsters who have surgical operations are more serious problems still. Dr. D. M. Levy studied the records of 124 children referred to him for grave fears and other maladjustments. All of them had undergone surgery. He found the most serious fears among the girls and boys who had been operated on before they were three years old. Their night terrors were particularly stubborn and gruesome. He recommends that, whenever possible, surgical operations be deferred until the child is at least three.

9. *Help your child develop skills to combat his sense of helplessness.* An eight-year-old friend of mine moved into a new neighborhood where most of the boys were a year or two his senior. They tormented him a good deal. They would

twist his arm, beat him up, and run him home. He was terrified to leave the house until his father taught him to box. After he passed out a black eye or two he became one of the boys. Anything you can do to make your youngster more skillful, builds his confidence; makes him more reliant, less subject to fear.

Geraldine —— was a gawky, unhappy youngster of fifteen who was afraid to go to birthday parties. Brought up to be seen and not heard, she was unsure of herself. Her parents, especially her mother, suppressed her; criticized her continually. "My, what a clumsy girl you are! Must you drop everything? Why can't you be like Amy?" The child withdrew deeper and deeper. Once the mother saw the error of her ways, she made amends. Geraldine got a permanent. Geraldine got much praise. Geraldine got a lovely new party dress. They gave her dancing and elocution lessons. And of course, Geraldine became a different person. Her new skills made her eager to try them out.

Anything you can do to make your child a distinctive, attractive individual helps to combat his sense of helplessness. The best time to begin is when he is still small. Under this plan he grows up with sturdy independence.

10. *Cultivate his confidence in you.* Always teach him that every thought in his mind may be talked about. Don't discourage him from speaking about any of his quandaries. You would be amazed if you knew the numbers of boys and girls who have to take their fears and worries about sex to a counselor because they say the subject is taboo at home. When he asks questions, answer them. Don't fall a-clucking and shake your head and say, "Naughty." Let your answers be simple enough for him to understand.

When he knows that you are a source of reliable information he will naturally think of you first whenever he is perplexed. He will not have to bottle up his curiosity; neither will he have to go outside the home to satisfy his curiosity. His sense of security becomes deep-rooted in you. And his fears diminish.

11. *Share your family problems with your child.* As an important member of the family group, he has a right to share in its hopes, ideals, worries, and problems. Even as a very young fellow he senses your fears and tensions. If you try to hide them, you only deepen his concern. How much more security you give him when you take him in as an active partner!

Of course you will not saddle him with your vague worries. You will talk, rather, about your problems in a realistic, calm way, when all of you are together. If father is called away to the armed forces, you will take Junior into your plans as soon as the news arrives. You won't withhold it until the day of parting.

If a baby is on the way, you will prepare him for the advent, far in advance. You will win him over, call it his and "ours," make him want to welcome it.

If father should lose his job, let Junior sit in on a family conference to lay plans for getting a better one. In all such crises, which most families have to face intermittently, always speak in hopeful, positive, constructive terms. In this way you help him to realize that life is made up in part of serious problems to be faced courageously. Don't keep him in an ivory tower. Let him take his rightful place in the family phalanx. Advance in a united front to meet your fears, head on—together.

12. *Teach him to believe in God.* Not a God of fear and vengeance. But a God of love and protection. Teach him something about the wonders of nature; the vast distance of the stars; the meaning of prayer and kindness. Let him see and hear you offer thanksgiving before your meals. Teach him when he is very young to say his prayers. Make certain

that his Sunday-school teacher is a wholesome, well-adjusted person, one who believes in a gentle, forgiving God. Teach him beyond everything else that all of us at times need more strength than is found within us. That at such times God is a safe refuge and comfort. This too will be a grand contribution toward his growing up to be fearless.

# 12.   Grow Out of Fear of Poor Health

OF ALL THE MARVELOUS medical discoveries, none is so arresting as *psychosomatics*. This big word of recent vintage refers to the interplay of the mind and body and their reactions on health. Commonly, it means that our ways of thinking can promote good or poor health, according to the kind of attitudes we hold.

Plato, the great philosopher of Athens more than two thousand years ago, predicted psychosomatics. He wrote, "For this is the great error of our day . . . that physicians separate the mind from the body."

Let's stop to consider what psychosomatics really means. It means that we can make the body sick as the result of inner tensions or thinking fearful, negative thoughts. It means also that our minds can spur the body back to health through wholesome attitudes. This is not mere metaphysical speculation; this is the conclusion of the latest researches in the field of medicine.

Dr. Edward Weiss and Dr. O. Spurgeon English of Temple University's School of Medicine write in their book, *Psychosomatic Medicine*, "In spite of the enormous incidence of cardiovascular disease, *the majority of patients who have symptoms referred to the heart region do not have evidence of organic disease.*" These distinguished authorities describe "organ language," whereby fears, tensions, and hostilities translate themselves into symptoms attached to this or that part of the body.

As you know, next to heart disease, cancer is the greatest killer of Americans. Today a vast, concerted effort goes on everywhere to unlock the mysteries of cancer. One of the most pregnant studies of that dreaded disease was reported at a recent meeting of the American Association for Cancer Research.

Dr. Philip M. West of the School of Medicine, University of California (Los Angeles), Dr. Eugene N. Blumberg, clinical psychologist at the University of Southern California, and Dr. Frank W. Ellis in charge of the tumor service at Long Beach, California Veterans Administration (where the study was conducted) teamed up to try to answer this question: Why is it that the same type of cancer may grow like wildfire in one individual and kill in a short time, whereas in another its growth is very slow and even stationary, the patient living for several years?

Here is their main conclusion: Fast-growing, fast-killing cancers are associated with personalities unable to find relief from their fears and inner tensions.

Dr. West, who reported the findings before the annual meeting of the Association in 1952, outlined a psychological approach. He and his colleagues studied the personality characteristics not only of patients with cancers of unusually rapid growth but also, for comparison, of those whose disease progressed very slowly in relation to the average for any type of cancer.

They gave the patients in both groups many psychological tests. However, they based their conclusions on only the best-known of the tests, *The Minnesota Multiphasic Personality Inventory,* "because the results are objective in scoring and interpretation and it may be easily repeated for verification by other researchers," Dr. West said.

He reported:

Significant differences in personality were found by the test between the two groups of patients. The findings suggested that the person with a rapidly growing tumor has a strong tendency to conceal his feelings and is less able to reduce tensions by doing something about them and "getting them off his chest" than is the person with the slowly growing tumor.

The results so far indicate that there are very definite personality patterns in cancer patients which can be correlated with an accuracy of 88 per cent with the relative rapidity of slowness of cancer progression in the individual patient and that this may have a strong bearing on the controllability of the disease by medical efforts.

It appears possible in many cases, therefore, to predict at the beginning of a malignant disease, long before the patient or the doctor can have any idea of the future course, how the patient will respond to treatment, and how rapidly or slowly his tumor may grow.

Dr. West also pointed out that Hodgkin's disease is one type of cancer, for example, from which some patients have died in a few weeks while others have lived for twenty years.

One patient with a stomach cancer may live only a short time after the onset of the tumor in spite of the best early diagnosis and treatment, whereas another may survive for many years even when the original cancer could not be totally removed.

A partial solution may be hidden in the emotional make-up of the individual. It seems reasonable that *the* *mind and the body are as much one functional unit** in cancer as in other diseases, such as stomach ulcer, colitis, hypertension, where psychological mechanisms have become increasingly prominent.

It is commonly accepted that the emotions can markedly influence the body defenses against disease and that the course of illness, even in infections such as tuberculosis, can be remarkably influenced by emotional stresses.

If space permitted, we could present similar conclusions of studies and conclusions made on patients suffering from asthma, certain allergies, stomach and duodenal ulcers and many other diseases. The general conclusion holds in every case: that fear-ridden, tension-filled individuals are afflicted with more ills of the body than those who resolve their fears and tensions; that recuperation from surgery, illness, and disease is accelerated by emotional adjustment. To put it more simply, peace in the heart is the best insurance against poor health; the best aid to getting well.

And so, our problems boil down to the prevention or solution of fears and inner tensions. Of course, no one is born with fear of poor health. Rather, all of us are born with a strong urge to live lustily; to have good health.

Why then are there so many hypochondriacs among us— those unhappy ones who go through life imagining all sorts of illnesses, aches and pains? (A definition I like better was given me by my friend Douglas Lurton: "A hypochondriac is a fellow who's looking for a hernia for his truss.")

Sometimes, of course, the lingering illness and death of a loved one turns us toward morbidity. Mrs. Y. can't rid her mind of the thought that she has cancer. She saw her sister die from it. Although Mrs. Y. gets a periodic check-up, she even doubts her physician's sincerity at times. She has been heard

---

* The italics are the author's.

to remark, "He probably says I'm all right just to quiet my mind." And then her common sense comes to the rescue and she admits that her imagination is too active.

Or take the case of Smith. His father died of cancer of the prostate gland. Recently, Smith discovered bleeding at the rectum and he was panic-stricken. Having an important business engagement that day, he deferred going to his physician. Next day his fear was dispelled when the physician assured him that a superficial vein had ruptured and that he need have no fear. A bit of unguent cleared up the difficulty immediately.

In such cases the best thing to do is get busy. Smith lived in great anguish until he went to the physician to get the facts. Mrs. Y. would be better satisfied if she visited several physicians for a check-up; if she told them nothing about her doubts; if she just got the facts from various reliable sources. For these, telling the same story, should remove the doubt in her mind. Moreover, Smith and Mrs. Y. can help themselves by shifting their thoughts into positive channels. If they need psychological counseling, the earlier they get it the better. Whatever course of action they take will certainly be preferable to living with their dread born of ignorance.

But Mrs. Y. and Smith are exceptional cases of hypochondria. For the majority of hypochondriacs get that way in their early childhood. Some children, as the result of a series of childhood diseases, become preoccupied with fears of chronic poor health. Often they hesitate to give up the attention and pampering received when they were actually ill. In later life, as responsibilities become heavy for them, they long to return to the days when they were tenderly nursed and protected.

Many hypochondriacs, because they are frustrated, turn to imaginary poor health as a way to attract attention. We have all been bored with the line of conversation of the typical hypochondriac. Whether it turns to indigestion, insomnia or a "needed" operation, it is at bottom a means of attracting attention, a kind of spotlight for the ego.

Other hypochondriacs grow up in an atmosphere of fear, worry, and anxiety—in homes where poor health is a sort of fetish. As you study the background of these hypochondriacs you are often impressed with a common element in their early lives. As youngsters the anticipation of poor health or disease is actually suggested to them by their parents. They hear constantly in their most impressionable years such warnings as:

"Come back into the house this minute, before you catch your death of cold!"

"Don't ever eat that, you'll get indigestion!"

"Come here, let me feel your forehead to see if you have a fever."

"You don't look well today, son; are you sure you feel all right?"

Not long ago I visited some friends who have two boys, five and seven years old. The older boy came running into the room and said, "Mummie, it's four o'clock. You haven't taken my temperature yet today!"

These boys come from excellent stock. They've had the best of care. Their diet is chock-full of vitamins A to Z. They spend a lot of time out of doors. Why do they have more colds and indispositions than their friends, many of whom are relatively neglected? I suspect that the two sons of my friends have more sieges of this or that kind of illness than their classmates because of an attitude they've been "taught." They expect to be sick rather than well. They are headed for hypochondria.

Of course, you may rightly protest that all children have to be warned to take care of themselves—to guard their health and be taught good health habits and hygiene.

You may recall two brothers in your acquaintanceship,

reared in the same home, who turned out quite differently. One grows up to be a man with healthful thoughts and rugged health. His brother, however, develops into a hypochondriac, although he too is never really ill.

If you gather all the facts about them you may find that the second one had a severe childhood sickness that left him below par for a time. After he fully recovered, his mother's repeated warnings developed his fear of sickness.

One of our first responsibilities, therefore, is to provide our children with a wholesome emotional environment. Let's teach them that good health is so natural and right that we should always expect it.

Another thing we can do for our youngsters and for ourselves is to teach and practice good health habits. Moderation in diet, exercise, work, and play is one of the best panaceas. When we set the habit of moderation early in life we protect our health then and in the later years.

Perhaps we should also think more often—with deep gratitude in our hearts—of the huge advances in preventive medicine. Our life span has more than trebled since Julius Caesar's day, has leaped ahead by 50 per cent since the Civil War because, in part, of the prevention of many diseases. Smallpox, diphtheria, yellow fever and many other old-time killers have been wiped out in America.

Joel Edwards recently expressed gratitude for the advances in modern medicine in an ariticle in *Coronet*. His wife had a bad cold and her nose turned a fiery pink. It was nothing really alarming until suddenly the pain became unbearable. He rushed her to a physician, who took a quick look at her, said *"Hmmm"* and gave her an injection. He asked her to return in three days.

As they were leaving, Edwards asked the physician, "What is it?"

"Nothing much," the doctor said. "Erysipelas."

When Edwards got home he looked *erysipelas* up in the dictionary. The frightening words *often fatal* bothered him. He hurriedly called the physician, who said, "Your dictionary's out of date. It must have been published before penicillin." Then he became serious. "At that," he said, "your wife's very lucky. If she had gotten erysipelas ten years ago she might have been a goner!"

Some of the most admirable men and women in history became great in the process of growing out of poor health. They had to keep occupied to escape their aches and pains. Robert Louis Stevenson, early smitten with tuberculosis, actually threw it off through hard work. (He died of a brain hemorrhage.) After a bad siege, he wrote to one of his friends, "By all the rules this should have been my death; but after a while my spirit got up again in a divine frenzy, and has since kicked and spurred my vile body forward with great emphasis and success."

Charles Darwin lived to a ripe old age because he lost himself in his work. His dyspepsia returned just as soon as he had time to think about it. Yes, wholesome escape from real or imagined illness is often an excellent way to lose the fear of poor health.

Just now we are all likely to be especially aware of the physically handicapped. So many of our boys have returned from the war with disabilities. Their big problem of adjustment is mainly psychological, because once they decide to live *with* rather than to fight the handicap, they are on the road to achievement and happiness.

Morbid brooding is a mental, not a physical, handicap. If your body is whole you of course have more "tools" available than you do if some of them are missing. But skill doesn't depend on the number of tools available. It depends on the use you make of those you have. It is the brain that directs the use of your tools, and your heart and mind give you the courage and ingeniousness to use them.

Commander Erle Cocke, Jr., of the American Legion, recently recounted the experience of Charley McGonegal who lost both arms in the war. Charley was watching a linotype operator setting type by machine. "Let me try that thing," said Charley eagerly.

The operator looked worried as he stepped aside for Charley to take his place at the machine.

"Don't worry," Charley said, "people can only be handicapped from here up—" He gestured with one of his hooks across his collar.

Within a few minutes the operator exclaimed, "By golly! That's better than people with hands can do first crack at it!"

Charley demonstrated, as have countless other unsung heroes, that the will to learn is the important thing. Psychologists since Adolph Adler refer to it as *overcompensation*.

Adler studied the lives of famous painters and discovered that many of them suffered from defects of sight. In their eagerness to make up or *compensate* for their deficiency they trained themselves to use what vision they had more carefully than do most of us with normal vision. They actually transformed their handicap into a gift.

And so it was that the deaf Beethoven was able to compose some of the greatest symphonies, and the blind poet John Milton and the blind Cardinal Newman to write deathless poetry.

Last year more than 140,000 seriously disabled veterans found jobs through the Civil Service in business and industry. Blinded veterans are now earning full salaries—doing as good work as workers with full vision—in wiring electronics machines, building television sets, and countless other highly skilled work. Handless veterans are running intricate machines.

And so it goes also with those suffering from the crippling effects of diseases, such as infantile paralysis and cerebral palsy. One of our biggest problems is to get rid of the handicaps in the minds of the public. For the vast majority of those who experience the loss of limbs or senses or co-ordinations learn to compensate, learn to live with their problems in happiness and contentment.

In the broad view, aren't we all handicapped? Since no one is perfect, each one of us must grow out of his limitations, must learn the vast potentialities that lie within him, and then tap them.

Let him who is confronted by poor health or disability look on two alternatives. The one is the bleak picture of self-pity, fear, surrender; the other is the road of reality and accomplishment. The signpost reads, "What do I do next?" The latter way may take a while to adopt. There will be dark hours of fear and despair, but eventually the second way is chosen by most.

Within the last few years many of us have read (and seen on the screen) *Cheaper By The Dozen* and *Belles on Their Toes*. These two delightful books, as you know, were written by two of the twelve children of Frank and Lillian Gilbreth.

Frank Gilbreth was one of the early pioneers in efficiency engineering. For many years he kept records of men and women with all kinds of physical disabilities who compensated for them in a distinguished way. Then when someone complained that he feared he would never be able to "overcome" his handicap, Gilbreth would pull out a "winning" case history of someone with the same handicap. That usually put a stop to whining and gave hope to the one who needed it badly.

To grow out of fear of poor health and disabilities, there is no better way than to look at the records of those heroes and heroines who "have done it." They and their experiences give the best inspiration and guidance.

# 13.  Rout the Fear of Losing Your Job

WHAT DO YOU WANT OUT OF LIFE?" is a remarkably useful question to ask anyone who fears losing his job. He invariably gives you as an answer a job-description quite different from the job he holds. Ordinarily he is in a line of work for which he has little stomach. And just as soon as he honestly answers "What do you want out of life?" he takes the first step in facing vocational realities. In that way he puts himself on the first rung of the ladder of job success.

That the successful man doesn't fear losing his job is a truism worth pondering. For there is usually a demand for the successful man's services.

In times of more workers than jobs—in the professions as well as the vocations—you ordinarily have to be efficient to get a job, to hold it, and to gain promotion. Efficiency is so necessary if you want to succeed that it becomes a psychological barrier for many. That is, we fear we aren't capable enough. At times the odds seem against us. So many people around us seem to get more things done than we do.

The busy physician sometimes doubts his efficiency when he reads an article in the medical journal by a colleague of his. "How does he do it, with that busy practice of his? Where does he find the time for research or writing?" And then he may begin to depreciate his own abilities.

A salesman I know is doing a good job in a Class III territory. He wonders whether he will ever be efficient enough to be promoted to a Class II or Class I territory. On the days that customers don't buy from him, he begins to feel panicky. He doubts his abilities, which are very real and admirable.

Or take the office secretary. The boss becomes angry at her for some mistake that anyone might make. Although she keeps back the tears, grave doubts flit across her mind. What if she should be fired? Right now she would be sorely embarrassed without a steady income. There's that fur coat to pay off and her mother is partly dependent upon her for support. . . .

Whenever we have experiences like the physician, the salesman, or the secretary, we doubt that we chose the right vocation. We are blue. We fear all sorts of woes that *might* fall upon our heads if we were to lose our job. Almost everyone feels this kind of fear from time to time. So long as it comes and goes occasionally it is perhaps good for us. It helps to keep us on our toes. It makes for a certain amount of healthy dissatisfaction, that goad to personal growth and accomplishment.

The fellow who constantly fears losing his job ordinarily feels inadequate. He may lack preparation for the job. He may not be interested in it. It may exceed his capacities or education. Or he may be bored because his job isn't challenging enough. He may have got the job through favoritism and consequently feels guilty about it. Such reasons as these may be real or imagined. But a hundred and one other reasons might be listed. Be sure of it: there's a good reason why he fears losing his job.

Many of us fail to face the question (What do you want out of life?) fair and square because we fear to give our definition of success. That is, we hesitate to advance a definition different from that held by our family, friends, and associates. We learn such hard and limited rules of success that when we interpret them in an individual way, we are likely to feel guilty.

Many of us define success in terms of worldly goods only. A man may crucify himself on the cross of a distasteful job simply to get the shiny car, the big home, and the tuition for a private school for his child. The shiny car, the big house, and the tuition may all be definitions of success in the eyes of his neighbors. Yet if he pays too high a price for them, no one knows better than he that they are specious definitions.

Torn between his job dissatisfaction on the one hand and his determination to succeed according to a stereotyped definition of success on the other, the fearful one either breaks down or spends his life in anguish and frustration.

An example or two may help to make my point clear. A college instructor of physics felt unhappy in his work. He was grouchy with his associates. His classes bored him almost as much as his students. He had worked hard to get his Ph.D. His parents actually made sacrifices to put him through college. Unwisely, they forced him into physics simply because his uncle had done so well in that field of research.

His first three years of teaching passed well enough. He was learning the ropes. The novelty of his position masked the tough going over the years. Moreover, that period coincided with his courting and marriage, a happy distraction. At the end of his first three years on the job, he was granted tenure. He had a job for life!

After that his teaching duties began to pall on him.

When we asked him what he wanted out of life, he said, "If I told you, you'd laugh at me!"

He wanted very much to devote his life to hunting and

fishing. We agreed that hunters and fishers must surely have a lot of fun if they like hunting and fishing. We asked him how he might turn his deep interest in the out-of-doors to vocational use. This started him on some systematic inquiry.

Eventually, he got a job in the North Woods for a summer as a camp guide. In the fall he took a sabbatical leave from the college, and he and his wife stayed in the North Woods.

They liked it. All during the winter he made trout flies; she wove rugs. In the spring they rented a camp and ran it with success. Today they have their own camp and are making a comfortable living. They are leading a happy and successful life. They're getting what they want out of life.

Another example: A successful salesman was invited to move to the home office as a line executive. The new position carried more prestige and a lot more money. But he turned down the offer.

"I have what I want," he said. "I love my home; my wife loves it. Over the years my customers and I have become friends. I'd hate to give them up. Our youngsters are doing well in school. They have their friends. They like their teachers. Why should I leave all this for *Ulcer Gulch* at the home office?"

Blessed is the man who knows what he wants out of life!

Another attack on this common fear of losing one's job is to get some expert vocational guidance, Isn't it regrettable that we are so niggardly in providing funds for vocational guidance in our schools and colleges? I daresay that our educators spend more on the teaching of foreign languages than on helping youngsters to find the right vocation.

Foreign language study is of course important for some, but not nearly so basic to the happiness of most of us as is competent vocational guidance. One reason I plug for more vocational guidance of the competent sort is that it so frequently is the right solution to fears about loss of job.

*The Dictionary of Occupational Titles* lists the names of more than 20,000 kinds of jobs whereby Americans earn a living. Out of this amazing number everyone of us is likely to find several to meet his individual needs.

One common reason why we fail to find the right niche is that we are often ignorant of the many kinds of jobs available. Another is that we know remarkably little—many of us—about our specific aptitudes and interests.

Let's assume that someone in fear of losing his job begins by answering the question, "What do you want out of life?"

Once he has obtained the answer—by himself or with aid—he may want to take another step; find out what his strengths and weaknesses are. One good way to do this is to put himself in the hands of an expert in vocational guidance.

His experience will then follow a pattern somewhat like this:

1. He will tell the vocational counselor that he is afraid of losing his job and that he would like some help.
2. The vocational counselor will talk with him to estimate him as a person—to get an appreciation of his background —and will probably suggest that he take some aptitude tests.
3. These tests will then be selected to cover the measurement of his (a) interests (b) mental capacities and abilities (c) personality and temperament (d) muscular co-ordinations and dexterity.
4. The tests will probably take him ten to twelve hours to complete. (This testing business must be done thoroughly. Otherwise it isn't helpful.) He will probably not be allowed to work on the tests more than two and a half or three hours at a time.
5. When he has completed the tests and they are scored and the vocational counselor has had an opportunity to study

the results, he will be given an interview. During the interview the vocational counselor will interpret the test scores for him.

6. The vocational counselor will then probably suggest that he read up on two or three vocations recommended to meet his indicated needs. He will be assigned specific references to read, such as *Occupational Outlook Handbook*. (This handbook is issued periodically by the United States Department of Labor in co-operation with Veterans Administration.)

7. He will then report to the vocational counselor for discussion based on his reading. At this time perhaps the individual's husband, wife, or parents may be brought into the picture. The idea is to base the choice of a vocation realistically, to avoid all foreseeable barriers.

8. The next step may be further education for the selected vocation. Or the vocational counselor may recommend an agency whose specialty is to place people in jobs.

9. I would recommend a further step. Once the individual is placed in the job for which he is fitted, he ought to report back occasionally to the vocational counselor for a check-up—to make sure that he is progressing as he should. I recommend this last step particularly for the man (or woman) who has suffered from the fear of losing his job.

To make sure that the vocational counselor knows his business and his credentials are approved, you may want to consult the list maintained by the National Vocational Guidance Association. This list, revised periodically, is available in most public libraries.

F. Kenneth Brasted, director of education of the National Association of Manufacturers, recently reported a dozen different reasons why people lose jobs. Please note that none of them is related to technical ability. Here is Mr. Brasted's list: (1) laziness, (2) disloyalty, (3) intemperance, (4) un-progressiveness, (5) poor personality, (6) emotional instability, (7) dishonesty, (8) immorality (defined by Mr. Brasted as irresponsibility to the family), (9) talkativeness (unkind gossip), (10) bad disposition, (11) poor health, (12) poor income management. Every one of us can do something about such handicaps.

Of course there are many other things we can do to minimize or expunge the fear of loss of a job. One of the finest things we can do is to improve our human relations. In a recent survey of 60,000 personnel problem cases, it was found that the majority of employees failed on jobs because of inability to get along with others, poor human relations, and defective personality characteristics. The breakdown is as follows:

| | |
|---|---|
| Lack of skill | 2.2 per cent |
| Inexperience | 1.0 per cent |
| Too slow in learning | 2.0 per cent |
| Carelessness | 3.0 per cent |
| Misdemeanors | 3.0 per cent |
| Personality | 88.8 per cent |

The Carnegie Foundation, in a study of 10,000 employed people, found that the reasons for most successes are as follows:

| | |
|---|---|
| Technical training and specific skills | 15 per cent |
| Personal qualities | 85 per cent |

Dr. Lawrence F. Greenberger, Director of Personnel Training at Kaufman's, Pittsburgh's largest department store, reports still another significant study. The study covered seventy-six corporations and revealed that 90 per cent of discharged personnel are released because of undesirable personal qualities, and 75 per cent of persons who are not promoted are held back because of poor personal characteristics.

Sometimes logic comes to the rescue of those who fear losing their jobs. Thoughts like these often help:

(1) Your employer can't operate without help.
(2) You were hired because someone was needed to do the work you're doing.
(3) If you not only do what you're required to do but give good measure, you're proving yourself unusual and valuable to the firm.
(4) If you have studied your work and do it as efficiently as possible, you'll be noticed and appreciated.
(5) If economic conditions are such that your job is discontinued, or the company goes out of business, your worry will have done no good.

Those who fear losing their jobs, as a group, worry about making a mistake. Everyone of course makes a mistake once in a while. Try to avoid it, but if you've made one, admit it quickly, frankly, and see what can be done to correct it. The fact that you take quick steps to avoid any serious results from a mistake will be remembered long after the mistake itself is forgotten.

A common cause of fear of losing one's job is slow promotion. Try not to be disturbed if your progress in the business world is slower than you think it should be. While there are exceptions, most of the really great achievements in the world aren't made by young people. J. Fenimore Cooper was forty-eight years old before he wrote his first book, yet his *Leatherstocking Tales* became classics. Henry Ford was nearing the half-century mark when he first rolled a car along a road under its own power. Elias Howe was about the same age when he perfected the sewing machine. It takes time to acquire the knowledge necessary to great accomplishments. If we will make sure that we are gaining knowledge in our field all the time, our future will take care of itself.

Think of it, almost nine out of every ten people in higher positions lose their jobs because they are hard to get along with. They are too emotional—too ready to fly off the handle. They just don't know how to work happily with others. Therefore, if we fear the loss of our job, perhaps a good place to begin to set our house in order is to check up on our human relations. If we are like a prima donna, perhaps we need help to get our attitudes and emotions straightened out.

There is an old Hindu saying: *When a student is ready, a teacher appears.* And so, if we really want to change our ways of dealing with others, we will have no difficulty in finding help.

Another thing we can do is make ourselves so valuable on the job that the boss will want to keep us. When we make ourselves virtually indispensable, we have no reason to fear being fired. The way to do this is to increase efficiency, to do more than just enough.

Still another thing we can do is find out how we stand with the boss. Make a friend of him. Let him know you're interested in your job, in him and his leadership, and in your company. Be enthusiastic about your work. Be proud of it. Ask him from time to time, "How am I doing?" Encourage him to rate you. Ask him for help to make you more valuable in your job.

If he is a good boss, nothing will make him admire you more. All of us like to know where and how we stand with the boss. It builds up our sense of security. If he indicates where we are unsatisfactory, we can take corrective measures. If he says that we are doing top-notch work in every respect, so much the better. In either event we know where we stand.

And that is one of the best ways to overcome fear of losing our job.

Now, suppose that the boss falls down on his job of being a good boss. Suppose that he will not give you the satisfaction of knowing how you are doing, and how you stand with him.

In that event, I believe you should give serious consideration to changing your job. Don't spend your life working for a sadist or an incompetent. While holding on to your job, look around for another. Make use of the classified advertisements, employment agencies, and tips from friends and relatives. In a systematic way look for a better job—one supervised by a good boss. In other words, if you have a poor boss where you are working, get yourself a good boss by changing your job.

Select if possible a company of excellent reputation—one that succeeds because of its care in selecting bosses of high caliber. Once you get a good boss, do right by him and the company. Give them your loyal co-operation and then you need not fear losing your job. One word more: while the fear of losing one's job is prevalent among workers of all ages, it occurs more frequently among those beyond middle age.

Here are some comforting facts for those in that category. Within the last five years American business and industry have revised their attitude about the older worker. He is again in demand. And the prospects indicate that he will continue to be in demand. I say this fully aware that many companies have pension plans and union contracts that prevent them from employing older workers.

Just recently the Prudential Insurance Company has extended the retirement age for women office employees from sixty to sixty-five years. Other large companies are following suit.

There are a number of reasons why we need older workers.

For one thing our population is constantly growing older. For another, our national indebtedness is so vast that we shall have to work longer to help pay it off. That is why so many retired men and women are going back to work. They have to help fight inflation.

Consider these comforting facts recently released by the Statistics Division of the Metropolitan Life Insurance Company:

Employment is at its highest for men between the ages of 25 and 54, when all but 5 per cent of them are working. At the older ages, although employment falls off, 56 per cent of all men are still working at ages 65–69. Even at 70–74 years almost 40 per cent are in some gainful activity. Not until the ages past 75 does the proportion employed drop below 20 per cent.

Fear about losing one's job often comes to the man who is forced into retirement at sixty-five or seventy, even if he has a pension. The pension may not be enough to meet inflationary prices. Let him know that there are other jobs awaiting him if he really wants to work. The jobs may be in an entirely different line from his life's work. And that may be an exciting adventure, if he will look on it that way.

As an instance I'd like to tell you about Mr. X. At seventy he was retired from his lifelong job as Y.M.C.A. secretary. His wife became ill, and his pension no longer met their financial needs.

He looked for a job. It took him three months to find one. It was selling mutual investment shares. He had to take a sales training course. This he enjoyed immensely. After he finished the course, he was given a territory. For three months he didn't make a sale. He was beginning to get discouraged because his earnings were principally dependent upon commissions.

And then things began to happen. Through his persistence

and eagerness to help others with their investment problems he began to make sales. Today at seventy-three years of age he is averaging $2,000.00 a month from his commissions!

An unusual case? Not from where I sit. One of the many grand things about these United States of America is the vast opportunity available to all of us at all ages.

This too is a source of comfort to those who fear the loss of a job. For where there is a will, there is a way. And our blessed country provides the way—or rather, the ways.

# 14.  Don't Fear Love

THIS PAST LECTURE SEASON I spoke before a number of college and university audiences on Modern Marriage. The audiences were mixed. Many GI's and their wives were among them. After the lecture we had a question-and-answer period.

Invariably sex problems came up. I was amazed at the intellectual maturity of these young people. A quarter of a century ago, we would not dare to discuss such matters in public. Young people today realize that if they are to stave off divorce, if they are to make marriage succeed, they must know a great many facts that formerly were not readily available to them.

I believe we are entering on an extremely healthful period, psychologically. We are turning more and more to *oikology,* the science and art of building happy homes. I say this despite the alarming fact that roughly one out of every four marriages currently ends in divorce. Nevertheless, I believe that we have as many happy marriages (if not more) today as fifty years ago. We simply don't cover up the unhappy marriages as we used to do.

Today many young folks **are** realistic about facing the responsibilities of marriage. These couples are less romantic and more practical than in "the good old days." They realize that marriage has the best chance of success when both partners prepare themselves to make it succeed. Among other things they are interested in substituting knowledge for what used to be called *the mystery of sex*. They have got rid of many harmful inhibitions in this respect. Consequently, we are now able to talk about sex as a natural function of the body, like digestion.

At a recent Youth Forum sponsored by *The New York Times*, boys and girls discussed sex education and came to some remarkable conclusions: home is the best place for a child to receive sex instruction, but fathers and mothers are not equipped to give it; parents often get emotionally upset when confronted with questions about sex; home, church, and school should supplement one another in giving sex education. All this sounds like mature thinking.

A great deal of confusion about sex education exists today, principally, I believe, because we so often fail to define our terms. Answers to a three-year-old youngster's questions about where he came from constitute one side of sex education. (Mothers and fathers should be prepared to answer such questions as they arise.) Information given to a twelve-year-old girl about periodicity is sex education. (Mothers should give this information, supplemented by instruction in the girl's hygiene class.) Counseling given to a young couple about to be married includes sex education. (This is usually provided by psychologists, physicians, or clergymen.) There are, of course, many other sides to the whole subject.

We are likely to do a lot of good, therefore, when we provide each individual with sound sex education according to his or her specific needs as they arise; and harm when we foist too much sex education on those not ready emotionally or intellectually to receive it. This means that home, church, and school all have work to do to help children and adults resolve their fears and worries about sex.

The best reason I know for advocating the right kind of sex education is that if it isn't given, the wrong kind will be learned instead. At around three years of age the youngster begins to ask questions about where he came from. When you answer him in a truthful but casual way you set his mind at rest. If you were to get alarmed or threaten him, you would make him wonder why, thereby increasing his curiosity. You would also make him resentful and fearful.

At three years, and even before, his interest in his body and his playmates' bodies increases. He ordinarily handles his genitals, particularly when he is nervous or worried. Later on he will probably indulge in masturbation (his little sister also), since masturbation is natural and not harmful in moderation. If he is lectured about the wickedness of "self-abuse" or told lurid stories of boys going insane from masturbation, he may develop fear of sex.

Dr. Clarence W. Schroeder in an article, "Divorce in a City of 100,000 Population," analyzes why people get divorces. He discovers that divorced couples more frequently report ignorance about sex matters when they were sex-curious children than do happily married couples.

Some parents, because of their own deeply ingrained inhibitions, can't force themselves to talk about sex with their children. The least they can do is to get someone else to talk over the matter with the youngsters. However, they will be better parents and happier individuals if they will get expert help in removing their own harmful inhibitions. They can also provide their children with phonographic records that tell the story of birth, or books on the gestation process written especially for the various ages.

During adolescence, boys and girls need much sympathetic guidance, particularly girls. Sex is more personal to a girl. It involves more of her being—more of her psychic life. Man never ceases to stand in awe of women's miraculous ability to bear children. There is an aura about her sex. And so we ought to recall from time to time some of the aspects of sex-education that are often neglected in the education of women.

Dr. Edmund Bergler, a colleague of Dr. Sigmund Freud in his later Vienna years, has just written an interesting book, *Divorce Won't Help*. Here he says that "Between 80 and 90 per cent of all women are frigid, or at least to some degree sexually disturbed." By frigidity, he means the inability of the woman to enjoy sexual relations and reach the orgasm during the sex act.

Those who do marital-relations counseling hear a recurrent complaint from couples: they are not able to achieve orgasm simultaneously. It is usually the woman who is the less responsive partner. There are of course many reasons why this is so. And once these reasons are more widely understood, we can expect many more happy marriages.

One of the reasons there are so many frigid women today is premarital promiscuous petting or necking. I believe we are justified in coming to the general conclusion that today even the "good" girl pets. Girls, of course, have always allowed the boys to kiss them. But I question whether any recent era has surpassed ours in "hot petting." Today, anything short of coitus goes under the definition of "hot petting."

The average "good" girl does not lose her virginity before marriage, but her acceptance of petting as a common practice in her social life often leaves emotional scars that usually fail to appear until after she marries.

You see, if she really believes that "hot petting" is wrong (and she usually does), yet submits to it, she builds within her subconscious mind a feeling of guilt. This feeling of guilt may not disappear with marriage. It may grow. Her husband can't deal with it. It is too furtive. Once girls and women realize the danger that unwise petting holds for their future happiness, those who want to have a good marriage become more judicious.

That brings me to a very important point: Why don't mothers do a better job of winning their daughters' confidence? Some time ago a pretty girl of sixteen came to say she wanted to discuss a very personal question. She didn't know how to begin. She was obviously quite embarrassed. Finally she said, "I want to know how far I should let my boy friend go when he kisses me good night."

I said, "Before we try to answer it together, will you tell me why you didn't ask your mother?"

"Oh, Mother is a dear. She bought me this sheared beaver coat and this solitaire. She is going to send me to Florida next year, if I pass my courses, with my aunt as a chaperon. She is a wonderful woman, but I wouldn't any more think of asking Mother a question like that than I would try to fly to the moon."

I said, "I can't tell you how far to let your boy friend go when he kisses you good night. You are a woman. You are a mature person. You have got to decide that for yourself. But I will be very glad to help think the problem through with you. You have got to make the final decision, however."

So we drew a line down a piece of paper, and on one side we put all the reasons why she should let the boy go pretty far. I said, "Give me one good reason."

She said, "My roommate in junior college is the hottest petter on the campus and she is the most popular girl. She has as many dates as she wants." (A good reason, because all of us want to be popular.)

After putting down some other reasons in favor of petting, we went to the other side of the column. I gave her a number of facts from studies made by psychologists and sociologists, that girls who pet heavily before marriage have a very high divorce rate. I explained how heavy petting often results in the creation of a *ghost lover* in the girl's subconscious mind; how the future husband is not always able to compete with the ghost lover. I indicated that chastity remains one of the best guarantees of successful marriage, according to recent studies, particularly in women, and to a great but lesser extent in men.

I gave her the results of other studies, and I said, "Well, now, you make up your mind. It was very nice of you to come in, and I appreciate your confidence."

The next morning she called to say, "I have thought this over, I waked up during the night and thought about it, and I want you to know my decision. You treated me like an adult. I want to tell you."

"Well, what is your decision?"

She said, "I decided I want to have a good husband and a happy home life, and a couple of youngsters. I don't want anything to interfere with that, but I don't want to be a prude, and this is my decision. I am going to let my boy friend kiss me good night on the cheek. But from now on I am going to discourage all his exploratory instincts!"

Questions of the sort the girl asked are uppermost in the minds of adolescents. Rather than force conclusions on them, we do a much better job of education when we help them to order their own thinking. Given the facts in a mature way, adolescents inevitably arrive at wholesome conclusions. For they want to do the right thing.

Colleges and universities are doing much to prepare for successful marriage. According to Professor F. Alexander Magoun of the Department of Human Relations at Massachusetts Institute of Technology, almost 2,000 professors in 550 colleges and universities are now teaching 657 courses in marriage and family relations.

Some years ago Rita Halle conducted a survey and discovered that the divorce rate of college graduates is the lowest

—from one-eighth to one-twentieth of the divorce rate of the states in which the colleges are located. It seems that we shall have to increase the number of family-relations courses in the high schools, where there is a greater number of potential divorced men and women.

One of the common fears of women is that they will never be able to find a husband. Although the average American girl receives at least two proposals to marry before she reaches twenty, many American women never marry. In 1940, the U. S. Census figures indicate there were 100.7 men for every 100 women. Twelve years later that rather nice balance is disturbed because today there are 110 women to every 99.1 men. This means that approximately 7,500,000 American girls and women will probably never get husbands.

The situation seems to have a lugubrious future too, because somewhat more than 175,000 men die each year in excess of women's deaths. According to some authorities there is a greater reluctance among young men today to undertake the responsibilities of marriage. In other words, bachelorhood is growing in popularity. Also, women are longer lived, and the nation's increasing life span will continue to make them more numerous than the weaker, male sex.

How to deal with this fear of going through life without a husband? One way is to decide as early as possible whether you want to marry or have a career. Girls who say "I want to marry *someday* but I'll wait a few years and try a career first" run the risk of being passed by. Although many a woman has proved that she can make a success of marriage and a career at the same time, she is the exception to the rule.

Statistics show that most men take wives who are between eighteen and twenty-two. As women get older their marrying rate drops off precipitously. This doesn't mean that some women of all ages don't marry, for they do. (Widows, incidentally, have a particularly high remarriage rate.) But those who wait until they are past twenty-five may expect that a husband will be harder to find.

Another way to deal with the fear of not getting a husband is to develop an attractive, lovable personality. Many a homely woman gets her man because she is such a grand person to be with. Many a beauty doesn't marry because her male acquaintances fear her selfishness and disdain. You and I could name a dozen Hollywood queens (in one breath) who are on the treadmill between altar and Reno. Why? Because they are practically impossible to live with. The young man with a head on his shoulders wants to marry more than a pretty face.

May I hold up a finger of warning and a pleading hand? Make sure you want to marry rather than show your friends and relatives that you can get a husband. The reason I offer this gratuitous advice is that so many women have told me they never really wanted to marry. They married simply because they resented the implication that they couldn't attract a husband; or their parents nagged them into it.

Voltaire once said, "There are two kinds of fools: those that marry, those that stay single." Although he gave us rather harsh alternatives, he did us a service by pointing out that marriage is not a solution to all problems.

Marriage, when contracted by couples *fitted for marriage,* is perhaps the most satisfying of all human relationships. For others it is far from ideal.

The most successful marriages are based on physical, intellectual, and spiritual compatibility. Such compatibility depends upon many things. Among these I would list particularly but not necessarily in order of their importance:

1. A happy temperament and emotional maturity.
2. Ability and willingness to "talk out" problems with each other.

3. Many common interests.
4. An acquaintanceship of several years before marriage.
5. Similarity of religious beliefs.
6. An engagement of at least eleven months.
7. A publicly announced wedding ceremony.
8. A happy childhood with memories of a compatible mother and father.
9. Freedom from frigidity or impotence.
10. A source of steady income.
11. A desire to rear at least two children.
12. Chastity.
13. Educational and economic background similar to the partner's.
14. Vocational adjustment.
15. A place to live independently of relatives.

Now, you may say, this is a hard bill of particulars. It is. But if marriage is a worthy institution, it is worth high standards and careful preparation. I am willing to admit that occasional marriages turn out quite successfully although they may not adhere to prescriptions. For example, I know a couple whose marriage has succeeded in a grand way; yet neither the husband nor the wife had a happy childhood. However, in both instances they received psychological counseling before they married and this relieved their tensions, traceable to childhood.

Or you can look at it this way: Marriage means many things to many people. If you have an attitude toward marriage different from that held by the majority, you may have a successful marriage anyway as long as you can find a partner who shares your views.

You may know a married couple who share a dislike for children and refuse to have any. Yet from all appearances they are compatible and are making a go of their marriage.

Although sex is the commonest marital bond, perhaps as many as 10 per cent of all American marriages are so-called "white marriages." Sexual congress doesn't play a part in them. Yet many of these white marriages are otherwise happy in companionship and homemaking, and successful in staying away from divorce courts.

Inasmuch as sex is the commonest marital bond, most marital fears cluster around it. Fear of the first night, while not as prevalent as formerly, is sometimes felt by the groom as well as the bride. Even though they have kissed and petted during the courtship, they have apprehensions about ability to please the partner. The groom has been taught by popular literature and folk tales that he must be masterful, and he sometimes doubts his ability to live up to expectations. The bride is sometimes scared by old wives' tales that she will experience pain.

A physical examination before the honeymoon, a chat with the family physician, a sense of deference to the partner's sensibilities, the realization that technique must be learned—such common-sense steps and attitudes ordinarily dispel wedding night fears and pave the way for growing compatibility.

Women sometimes fail to respond in the sex act because their husbands do not arouse them sufficiently before coitus. The average man is rather clumsy in such matters. He is usually intent on obtaining immediate satisfaction. Yet the woman can do at least two things to make him a better lover.

First of all, she can put informative literature in his way. I often recommend Havelock Ellis' famous essay on love-play to men about to be married and to those whose wives complain of their technique. Men are only too eager to improve in this respect, once they are assured that it is possible.

The other thing the wife can do is to encourage her husband to love her tenderly. Many women are prudish. Perhaps their parents were too strict with them—supervised them too closely, or taught them that sex was bad. Some women, for example, will not tolerate a kiss below the neck. They are ignorant that the female body may develop erogenous zones —for example, on the neck or bosom—if they will permit their husbands to excite them.

Now let us talk about the most important cause of all—why husbands and wives are not equally responsive. That is usually self-centeredness. Take the wolf, for instance. The wolf is an emotionally sick man. He is a neurotic. He thinks only of his own gratification. (As a matter of fact, he usually doubts his virility and constantly tries to prove it to himself by chasing many women.) The nymph too is an emotionally sick woman. She is a neurotic, usually a narcissist. She thinks only of her own gratification. Her seeking of sex enjoyment with various partners is proof that she can't enjoy sex in the first place.

The wolf and the nymph are childlike emotionally. They have not learned that love springs from giving rather than taking. And they continue to lead frustrated lives until they learn that very precious lesson.

Can husband and wife *learn* to achieve orgasm simultaneously? Of course. Often they must change their whole attitude toward life. But if they are sincere in trying to think first of the partner's happiness they find that their love life grows in meaning and unison. Often they also need expert guidance.

It sometimes takes years. According to my case histories, I find that not until the seventh year of married life do couples find fullest harmony in their sex relations. When we understand that sex enjoyment results from many things, not the least of which are the kindly acts and thoughts of selflessness throughout the days, weeks, and years, we appreciate that sex adjustment is not always easy.

Husbands and wives sometimes fear pregnancy: husbands

for financial reasons usually; wives for physical reasons. Perhaps some self-addressed questions may help to locate the reason for the fear and therefore dispel or circumvent it.

1. Have we talked out the problem of having children? Are we agreed on whether we want children? How many? (According to a *Fortune* survey a few years ago, the average American wife would like to have twice as many children as her husband wants.) Since the basic purpose of marriage is to propagate the race, the best time to settle questions of this kind is before marriage.

2. When shall we have the first child?
   (Statistical studies show that those marriages are happiest that defer having the first child during the first two years, provided the first child arrives before the fifth year.)

3. Let us assume we could have a child during the first year; how can we delay its advent? (There are only three ways. The surest way of course is to practice incontinence. Another way is to use contraceptives, if your beliefs permit. A third way is to govern sexual relations according to the rhythm of the wife's ovulation. The family physician can provide expert advice about these matters.)

4. How can I allay my fears connected with carrying my first child? (Put yourself in the hands of an excellent obstetrician. Follow his advice. Be assured by your husband's tenderness and the great strides made in obstetrical science. If you feel that you still have an unreasonable fear about pregnancy, get some help from a psychiatrist or psychologist. Hold on to the thought that motherhood can be the most satisfying and blessed experience in a woman's life.)

Fear of pregnancy often is greatest among unmarried girls. As an example, I'd like to tell you about Mary, an adopted

child. She was reared in a luxurious home under strict conditions. She was seventeen when she came to see me. She was
deeply ashamed—found it hard to tell me that she was afraid
she might be pregnant. She told me how she had sought
companionship and understanding outside her home. She
said that she couldn't stand the shame; that she was contem-
plating suicide. She told me that her period was two days
overdue, that she had lived in agony ever since her first and
only sexual relations with her boy friend two weeks prior to
her visit to my office.

I reassured her that there were many ways to solve the
problem; that while she had made a foolish mistake there
was still a good life ahead for her. I assured her that I would
help. I said that I would be happy to talk with her foster
parents and her boy friend. I told her of the Florence Critten-
den League and its wonderful work in helping unmarried
mothers. And as we talked I could see her relax and take
heart.

"But," I said, "I'll be willing to bet that you aren't pregnant. Go home. Be certain that we will find a way out. Promise me that you will not repeat your mistake. And let me hear
from you in two days. By that time you and I will decide
which step to take."

The next morning at nine o'clock she telephoned from a
suburb. "Everything's all right!" she said.

Fear had taken such a hold on her that her body processes
were upset. Once she relaxed, her periodic cycle resumed.
Some time later she and the young man married, and they
now have a family and are getting along quite happily.

We must be more understanding and helpful in dealing
with unmarried mothers, and their children particularly.
The Europeans are wiser in this regard than we. However,
our insight is growing. The present popularity of adopting
children helps. For countless illegitimate children are being

adopted into good homes. But what about the mothers who give them up only because they fear the shame we would otherwise force upon them and their babies?

One of the most difficult fears to deal with is homosexuality. Fear of detection and fear of not being able to resolve it are present among many American males and females. The famous *Kinsey Report* estimates that approximately 4 per cent of the male population are overt homosexuals. Estimates from other sources put overt homosexuality among women at from 5 to 8 per cent.

Since society frowns upon overt homosexuality, which involves actual sexual contact with members of the same sex, millions of homosexuals have cause for fear and worry. Before they can be helped they of course must want to be helped. Their basic decision must be between two alternatives: Shall I learn to live with my homosexuality and face the possible consequences? Or, shall I seek help for its correction?

According to most authorities, the cause of homosexuality is almost always of psychological origin and can usually be traced to childhood, between the sixth and the eleventh years, as a rule. Through psychiatric therapy, homosexuality is often alleviated.

No one knows how much latent or subconscious homosexuality there is. But it must be more widespread than the overt kind. Some years ago a young married man came to see me about his heavy drinking. He was afraid that he might become an alcoholic.

After going into his background and giving him some psychological examinations, I asked to see his wife. She was an unusually beautiful woman who had been a professional model before her marriage. She talked freely and attributed her husband's drinking to dissatisfaction with his job.

She assured me that their sex relations were entirely satisfactory. She became interested in the psychological examinations that her husband had taken and asked if she might take some. I gave her the Rorschach Diagnostics, the ink-blot test. When we came to Card III she described the blot in this way: "I see two men. They're naked. No—I'd like to change that. They're pigs."

Then she described some other impressions and finally said, "I'd like to change that first statement again. They're not pigs, they're two beautiful girls dancing in the nude."

Later on, other of her responses were likewise significant.

When she returned in a day or two to discuss the results, I asked whether she wanted to change her report that sexual relations between her and her husband were satisfactory. She began to wipe tears from her eyes and said, "No, they're not. I always put on an act. I like my husband, and I want to stay married. But I don't like intercourse."

Eventually she filled in other significant details. Her mother had died shortly after her birth. From the time she was ten years old she lived with her father, who was a gambler and bootlegger. By the time she was fourteen her father's cronies "began to maul me" so that "I always hated men—the pigs."

Shortly after, she ran away from her father and became self-supporting. She roomed with various girl friends. She reported that they were very devoted to one another. That, while she experienced no overt homosexual acts with them, she "adored their company." When she married she couldn't understand her frigidity, because she liked her husband.

She was referred to a psychiatrist for deep therapy. Today she and her husband are happy and well adjusted. How many similar cases exist—instances of frigidity caused by unconscious homosexuality—no one knows. The important thing to remember is that such problems are commonly cleared up with expert help.

Countless other fears related to carnal love are the lot of many people: fears related to the menopause, to the male climacteric, to contamination, and the like. Yet each of them can be solved if the afflicted will only seek help and guidance.

There are certain common signs that tell us when we need help with our love problems. When we long for love but can't bring ourselves into contact with those who might give it— that is a sign. When we complain of the lack of opportunity to express or find love—that is another. A third is always being disappointed in love relationships—expecting too much from others, such as the man or woman who can't find a partner good enough to marry. A fourth sign is the quest for the perfect love or love situation through a series of sex relationships. These signs point to those who most often suffer from various fears related to love.

As they grow in understanding through expert guidance they learn that love has many manifestations. To be proud of oneself, one's attitudes and values—this is a wholesome kind of love. To be devoted and tender to a life partner through bad times as well as good—this too is a wholesome, a most satisfying kind of love. To spread attitudes of affection, kindness and understanding among the weak and unfortunate—this love usually springs in those who love (or have loved) another more dearly than self.

These three manifestations of love are among the highest expressions of the human personality. Those who have not experienced them lose much if they don't develop them. For where love blossoms, fear does not grow. Victor Hugo once said, "The greatest happiness of life is the conviction that we are loved, loved for ourselves— Say rather, loved in spite of ourselves." And Emerson emphasized, "Love and you shall be loved. All love is mathematically just—as much as the two sides of an algebraic equation."

# 15. Learn How to Control Fear of War and Battle

DURING THE FIRST World War, thousands of American soldiers chuckled over the "French soldier's philosophy." They liked it well enough to pass along to their buddies and the folks back home. It always brought a bit of consolation. It went like this:

There's no sense worrying about what's going to happen to you in the war. Either you'll be drafted or you won't. If you aren't drafted there's nothing to worry about. If you are drafted, one of two things will happen. Either you'll be sent to the front or you won't. If you won't be sent to the front, there's nothing to worry about.

If you're sent to the front, one of two things will happen. Either you'll be hit, or you won't. If you aren't hit, there's nothing to worry about.

If you're hit, one of two things will be true. Either your wound will be slight or it will be serious. If it's a slight wound, there's nothing to worry about. If it's serious, one of two things will happen. Either you'll recover or you won't. If you recover, there's nothing to worry about. And if you die you can't worry.

Many a poilu and doughboy remarked that this wry slice of logic put them in a fatalistic frame of mind that helped to dispel their fears of war and battle.

Today our military leaders are more alert than ever to the need to allay fears among the armed forces. For they realize that morale is priceless. It so often means more in winning a victory than equipment. Consequently, our military leaders have encouraged psychologists to help them study the fear of war and battle and come up with recommendations to control it.

Psychologist J. Dollard deduced from the experiences of three hundred recent veterans twelve rules for meeting battle fear:

1. Learn to know when you are becoming afraid.
2. Figure out in advance the best ways of meeting danger.
3. Keep remembering that being scared makes you a smarter soldier and a safer one.
4. Keep your mind on the job and do it a step at a time.
5. Don't forget that the enemy is scared of you.
6. Remember that your life may depend on somebody else's guts and his on yours.
7. Remember if you lose, the enemy wins.
8. Never show fear in battle.
9. Make a wisecrack when you can.
10. Fear wears you out, so forget it when you can.
11. Don't hesitate to talk about being scared.
12. Have a good time when you can; fun combats fear.

Lt. Colonel Evans F. Carlson (USMC), hero of Makin Island and Guadalcanal, was chiefly responsible for the spread of the *Gung Ho* idea among our fighting forces during World War II. He said, "When you hire American boys in any peacetime business, you use *all* they have to offer—their brains, their suggestions, their initiative. Then why, in the name of common sense, should we not run the business of war on the same basis?"

Some years before World War II, Evans Carlson was assigned to command a detachment of natives in Nicaragua. This detachment had killed its two preceding Marine Corps Officers. "I figured," he said, "those officers had been killed because their men feared or distrusted them. The officers didn't understand the people they were dealing with. I made up my mind to understand them. My Spanish wasn't too good, but from the first I never used an interpreter. I never punished a man, either, until I had been able to make him admit he deserved it. Before I left, those peons were bringing me their family quarrels to settle."

*Gung Ho* is one of the best antidotes for battle fears known to psychologists. It means working together, for the good of the group—co-operation. "*Gung Ho* was the yardstick," explained Carlson. "Any action was *Gung Ho* or it wasn't. To help a man out of a tight spot, to jump in and do anything that needed doing without asking whose turn it was to do it, that was *Gung Ho*."

The *Gung Ho* system worked because the officers and men knew one another intimately. Although many of them had never read Dumas' *The Three Musketeers,* they were unknowingly applying their motto: *All for one and one for all!*

"I wanted to know all about each of my men," said Carlson. "I wanted to know about his intelligence, adaptability, initiative. At the same time I wanted him to feel that he was more than a serial number to me. He was that certain individual, John Smith or Ignace Ponitowski, and if he passed muster we were going to do a job together—he and I."

One of the finest things Colonel Carlson did to minimize

fear was to organize *Gung Ho* meetings. He whipped up enthusiasm from the opening. He began the meetings with the Marine Hymn and the Star-Spangled Banner. Then he would talk to the men on a subject uppermost in all their minds, such as why they were fighting, patriotism, co-operation, how they could profit from their last campaign, what the plans were for the immediate future, how they could help each other to a greater extent. He threw the meeting open to questions and discussion. Any soldier, regardless of rank, was allowed to say what was on his mind. He could offer suggestions and make criticisms, provided they were constructive. For each man was an important guardian of the *Gung Ho* spirit.

Officers and enlisted men are closer together in the American armed forces today than ever before. They are a model for other countries. Behind it all is the democratic spirit, and nothing serves so well to dissipate fear in battle. Anything officers and enlisted men can do to further the *Gung Ho* spirit is a contribution to morale and inner confidence.

If I had the privilege of being a young soldier or sailor in the armed forces I believe I would do these things:

First, I would have a good talk with myself. I would admit quite frankly and freely that I had fears and misgivings, if I had them. I would be foolish if I didn't realize that war is and always has been a frightful business. I would certainly say to myself, "I am not ashamed to admit that I shall be afraid on more than one occasion. But I'm going to face my fears and learn the tricks of mastering them."

Second, I would enter upon my training with eagerness to learn my job so well that I could "do it from reflex action." I would learn to excel in bayonet practice, hand-to-hand fighting training, and the rest if for no other reason that I would then be in the best way to preserve my life (and my friends' lives) in an emergency.

I would give every co-operation to my trainers. I would

learn to obey commands explicitly, for I would realize that by doing so I would be buying life insurance.

Third, I would make friends of my messmates and officers. For I would realize that their affection and comradeship are excellent antidotes to fear. I would particularly cultivate at least one close friend with whom I could share my fears and worries. For by sharing them they shrivel.

Fourth, I would take an active part in as many entertainments and relaxations as I could. I would have as much fun as possible. The activity and happiness springing from these participations offer wholesome escapes from the hum drum and irritations of war.

Fifth, I would get as much rest as possible. And I would keep fit. For I realize that fear flees from a rested and healthful body.

Sixth, I would whistle and sing some part of each day. I would actively cultivate a buoyant, cheerful spirit. For a glad heart does not harbor fear.

Seventh, I would discuss occasionally with my officers and messmates the things I am fighting for. I would refresh my memory with the spirit of America. I would count over the basic freedoms that America cherishes and represents. I would remember that America is a peace-loving nation; that she fights only when her freedoms are threatened. I would take just pride in thinking, I am actually fighting for myself and my loved ones to help preserve the dignity of the individual against those forces that represent enslavement and repression.

Eighth, I would write regularly to those I left behind. I would help allay their fears, for I would feel proud of my strength of spirit. I would tell them of my love for them. I would share with them my plans for the future. I would let them know that I resolved my fears. I would praise my outfit.

Ninth, I would want to shoulder a just share of the responsibility to keep courage and morale high in my "outfit." Doing this, I would have a deep inner satisfaction and also I would soon be noticed as officer material. For such an attitude would be a sign of leadership.

Tenth, I would work hard to develop my sense of humor. I would try my best to overlook the minor irritations. I would laugh at myself more than at others. I would be quick to see the ridiculousness in an awkward situation. And I would refuse to hold a grudge. In this way I would keep the negative emotions under control.

Eleventh, I would plan for my future. I would learn all about the benefits due me upon being mustered out of the service. I would decide whether I wanted to continue my education. If so, where and how I would begin. If, instead, I wanted to return to my old job, get a new one, or start a business of my own—I would use spare minutes to think about these things. In my daydreaming I would think about my girl friend, about marriage and what I want out of life. Thinking along these lines is constructive; it nurtures hope and worthy goals. I would always remember this pyschological truth: The mind can accommodate just one thought at a time. Therefore, I'd keep my mind thinking a positive thought always.

Twelfth, I would think of my armed-forces experience as a grand opportunity to deepen my insight into human nature. I would be eager to study new faces, new voices, new customs, new languages. I would keep my eyes and ears open. I might even jot down a few notes occasionally—keep a kind of diary to refresh my memory in the years ahead.

Thirteenth, I would read—if for only a few minutes on those days when I had an opportunity to do so. I would carry with me a pocket edition of the Bible or other inspirational work. Whenever I would have access to a library I would look for a book that tells how other soldiers and sailors faced their fears—a book such as Stephen Crane's *The Red Badge of Courage*. I would project myself into the main character. I would then analyze his problems, his strengths and weaknesses. I would also read other books—whodunits, comics, whatever gives me pleasure.

Fourteenth, I would cultivate friendship with my chaplain. If I had been remiss about my religious observances, I would talk with him and renew them. I would recall such testimonials as this: "If I had not had a personal religious philosophy when I entered combat I do not believe that I would have lasted at all. For me it was most definitely a source of strength. I require no one else to hold my beliefs but I experience intense personal comfort from them myself. I can think of no other single thing that sustains me day by day so much as my personal belief in God."

Fifteenth, I would say at least one prayer every day, silently or aloud. It might be a prayer of my own; it might be the *Lord's Prayer* or one of the Psalms. Or, it might be a prayer like that of Saint Francis of Assisi:

> Lord, make me an instrument of your peace;
> Where there is hatred, let me sow love;
> Where there is injury, pardon;
> Where there is doubt, faith;
> Where there is despair, hope;
> Where there is darkness, light;
> And where there is sadness, joy.

> O Divine Master, grant that I may not so much seek
> To be consoled as to console;
> To be understood as to understand;
> To be loved as to love;
> For it is in giving that we receive;
> It is in pardoning that we are pardoned;
> And it is in dying that we are born to eternal life.

# 16.  Face the Fear of Death

HOW SHALL WE FACE the inevitable? That depends, it seems to me, on the individual and his outlook on life. When Woodrow Wilson was president of Princeton University he wrote an essay: "When a Man Comes to Himself." The point he makes, as I remember it, is that you have to arrive at a personal philosophy to lead a happy life. And the sooner you do it, the better your life is.

When our lives are full of purpose we are so busy in the pursuit of it that we don't have time to dwell on the melancholic aspects of death. And if our purpose is a worthy one we can take great comfort in making it come true. The best measure of a purpose is, "How much does it help others?"

The vast majority of us do lead wholesome, purposive lives. Our days are spent for the most part in helping others. The husband and father who loyally gives a good day's work for a good day's pay is a really heroic fellow. Occasionally he doesn't feel like going to work, but he goes nevertheless. Sometimes he is discouraged by the many problems that face him—worries about money, his job, his children's education, his wife's health. But he does keep on the job. He does meet his responsibilities. And by doing so, he proves himself to be a really noble man.

If he will only realize the great contributions he is making to his family and society; if he will only stop occasionally and review his accomplishments; if he will only take just pride in himself—he will be happy and confident. (Too many men and women "centered in the sphere of common duties" fail to give themselves enough pats on the back.)

In like manner, the wife and mother who does her job well —no matter how modest she may think the purpose of her life—is making a grand contribution of the selfless sort. If she will think from time to time how valuably the care and love that she bestows upon her family contribute to the welfare of the community and nation, she will realize that her life has purpose.

No one seems to know very much what natural death is. Dr. George W. Crile, late professor of surgery at Western Reserve University's School of Medicine, believed that death results from acidosis. He said that death is caused by the failure of the organism to maintain the alkalinity necessary to its normal functioning. And Sir William Osler, the "physician's physician," and his colleagues in the medical profession agree closely that regardless how painful its antecedents may be, death itself is entirely free from pain.

Camille Flammarion, for many years head astronomer at France's National Observatory, during the latter part of his life collected thousands of testimonials from eyewitnesses of death. He too reports, in *Death and Its Mystery,* that when death comes we are free from pain. This comforting thought is an aid to facing the fear of death.

All of us are naturally curious about death, as we should be, for it is the most baffling of all the phenomena in our experience. The Freudian psychologists believe that all of us experience subconscious if not conscious fear of death. Certainly all civilizations have left records of their concern about death.

The oldest book (papyrus) we have is the Egyptian *Book of the Dead,* a rather fascinating guide for the deportment of mummies in the afterlife. Greek and other mythologies, sarcophagi, and monuments all bear witness to mankind's sustained preoccupation with death. One of the biggest problems connected with it is how to reconcile ourselves to the loss of a loved one.

I once knew a woman of religious fervor who, when she lost her only son, cursed God and would have nothing more to do with religion. Obviously, her religion was of superficial depth. She devoted the rest of her life to mourning and bitterness. She cast a shadow across the many lives that came under her influence.

How different from one of America's great ladies of the stage, Helen Hayes! Her daughter, you may remember, was taken away suddenly in an epidemic of infantile paralysis. At the time, Helen was in a Broadway production. Laboring under her great tragedy, she continued to do her work. She plunged into a heavy schedule of overseas programs for the armed services. Through helping others she found release from her pain.

Loud and prolonged lamentations do not always relieve grief. Neither do they always reveal truest sorrow. The stoical attitude is more mature, as Plutarch's famous letter to his wife exemplifies:

> Plutarch to his wife, greeting. The messengers you sent to announce our child's death, apparently missed the road to Athens. I was told about my daughter's death on reaching Tanagra. Let me hope, that you will sustain both me and yourself within the reasonable limits of grief. What our loss really amounts to, I know and estimate for myself. But should I find your distress excessive,

my trouble on your account will be greater than on that of our loss. I am not a "stock or stone," as you, my partner in the care of our numerous children, every one of whom we have ourselves brought up at home, can testify. And this child, a daughter, born to your wishes after four sons, and affording me the opportunity of recording your name, I am well aware was a special object of affection.

—Plutarch

As civilizations ebb and flow, so do various attitudes toward death and survival after death. Here are ten attitudes that recur:

1. *Death is the threshold of a future existence.* Those who hold this idea believe in the immortality of the soul. They also believe that their own death will provide a reunion with those who have gone before.

2. *We survive after death only in the minds of others.* Therefore, it is our duty to lead an exemplary life, so that the memory of us will be cherished by those who come after. The Chinese have obtained much comfort from this point of view. Countless Chinese families preserve genealogies of their families going back more than a thousand years. Relatives of distinction are remembered on their birthdays with special observances. The devotion of the Chinese to their ancestors and families is their strong bid for individual immortality.

3. *Death is looked upon as the end of pain and frustration and is often compared to a deep sleep after a grueling day.* Pushed to a logical conclusion, a Schopenhauer would advocate suicide as a means of hastening one's escape from this dour outlook on life.

4. *Death is sometimes looked upon as an awakening after "life's fitful dream."* Those who have led a life of extreme

hardship—and have faith in personal survival—often hold
to this point of view. Many men and women who reach
great age and linger on in poor health frequently hold to
this idea of death.

5. *Because death is inevitable and because we probably
   shall not survive it, we had better eat, drink, and be merry,
   for the pleasures of the senses are real if fleeting.* This so-
   called Epicurean point of view is perennially popular, although it is ordinarily based on disillusion and selfishness.

6. *Death is a punishment for our sins ("The wages of sin is
   death") and through the punishment we find atonement.*
   This point of view seems to be on the decline at present.

7. *Death presents an opportunity to help others.* Acts of
   supreme heroism and martyrdom come under this category. ("Greater love hath no man than this, that a man
   lay down his life for his friends."—John 15:13) Many a
   soldier and sailor has demonstrated his belief in this point
   of view.

8. *Although death comes to all, some are predestined to survive it in Heaven; others in Hell.* This belief is held particularly by certain religious sects.

9. *Death marks a transition of the soul from one body to
   another. (Reincarnation.) The best thing to do, therefore, is to lead a good life so that the next incarnation will
   be on a higher plane than the present one.* This point of
   view is strong in India and other parts of the orient.

10. *Since death is inevitable, the best thing to do is lead an
    active, ethical life and not worry about it.* This stoical at-
    titude seems to be on the increase in America.

How each of us faces death or the fear of death depends
upon how we live and what we live by. Millions upon millions have lived and are living with a personal philosophy
based on each one of the ten points of view (and others). Yet

only the one we have faith in is worth very much to us individually. Of course, some of them lend themselves to blending. We can accept, for example, the second, the eighth and the tenth points of view without necessarily being illogical. But one of them is likely to mean more to us individually than the other nine.

I said that all civilizations have been concerned about death. In the Dark Ages, for example, many devoted large portions of their short lives to little else than pondering about death. Today the climate is different, particularly in America where we are stimulated into constant activity. That is why perhaps so many of us find a life of active duty one of the best ways to face the fear of death. We feel that a considerable part of the fear of death lies in dwelling upon it; that constant meditation upon death increases fear and tension, and therefore defeats its purpose. Observe those who think much about death and you find them ordinarily neurotic and short of affection. They are self-centered.

Psychologically, a good time to begin to face death is when you fear it. A good beginning might be the statement, "There's no use to try to run away or become hysterical about death. Each minute it comes closer. But, thank goodness, I don't know when I shall die. It may be today; it may not be for three-quarters of a century. And so, I'm just going to live a day at a time. When it comes, I'll take it in my stride as billions have done before me."

Once we face the stark reality we can do two other healthful things. We can decide not to bother ourselves any more about it. And we can keep busy on a program of self-development and help to others.

Such a course brings the most happiness to most men and women. If we believe that happiness is a poor value, then we will have none of the recommendation. If, however, we respect happiness and want more of it in our lives, we will get busy—whether we are twenty-one or eighty-one. We will get busy applying this recommendation because it's worth putting into action. We will use our common sense. We will realize that our dignity and happiness consists of our thoughts and attitudes. We will use them for worthy purposes, not to inflame the imagination.

Pascal once wrote, "If the greatest philosopher in the world finds himself upon a plank wider than actually necessary, but hanging over a precipice, his imagination will prevail, though reason convince him of his safety."

How often do we allow the imagination to sink us! A friend recently told me about a man whose lower limbs became numb. His physician diagnosed the condition as *Buerger's disease* and said that the lower limbs would have to be amputated eventually to prevent the onset of gangrene.

The man spent several days trying to make up his mind what to do. Each night he awoke from a nightmare. My friend counseled him to get other medical advice. At a famous clinic where the man was given thorough diagnosis, he was pronounced suffering from low blood pressure. Within a few weeks his legs were in excellent condition as the result of careful treatment.

Our fear of death so often stems from a rampant imagination. Let us use our reason, our common sense. Let us analyze our problems. Let us bring our unhappy experiences into the sunlight. Let us give up our dream worlds of fantasy. Let us do something about our fears. Let us keep in mind that "every day is a fresh beginning—every morn the world begins anew."

One of the best things we can do for ourselves, particularly in relation to fear of death, is to study the lives of our noble teachers. The Christ, the Buddha, Socrates, and many others taught and demonstrated ways to overcome the fear of death. We can turn to them for inspiration and guidance.

Next to the Christ, my favorite teacher is Socrates. His life was so full of self-development and help to others that when his death approached, it held no fear for him.

You will recall that the judges condemned Socrates to drink poison (hemlock) because of his teachings. His friends offered him a way to escape. But he refused. His students came to see their old teacher in jail, and after a short chat, he asked one of them, Crito, to have the poison brought in.

"Yet," said Crito, "the sun is still upon the hilltops, and many a one has taken the draught late; and after the announcement has been made to him he has eaten and drunk, and indulged in sensual delights; do not hasten then, there is still time."

Socrates said: "Yes, Crito, and they of whom you speak are right in doing thus, for they think that they will gain by the delay; but I am right in not doing thus, for I do not think that I should gain anything by drinking the poison a little later; I should be sparing and saving a life which is already gone; I could only laugh at myself for this. Please then to do as I say, and not to refuse me."

Crito, when he heard this, made a sign to the servant; and the servant went in, and remained for some time, and then returned with the jailer carrying the cup of poison. Socrates said: "You, my good friend, who are experienced in these matters, shall give me directions how I am to proceed." The man answered: "You have only to walk about until your legs are heavy, and then to lie down, and the poison will act." At the same time he handed the cup to Socrates, who in the easiest and gentlest manner, without the least fear or change of color or feature, looking at the man with all his eyes, as his manner was, took the cup and said: "What do you say about making a libation out of this cup to any god? May I, or not?" The man answered: "We only prepare, Socrates, just so much as we deem enough." "I understand," he said; "yet I may and must pray to the gods to prosper my journey from this to that other world—may this then, which is my prayer, be granted to me." Then, holding the cup to his lips, quite readily and cheerfully he drank the poison.

And hitherto most of us had been able to control our sorrow; but now when we saw him drinking, and saw too that he had finished the draught, we could no longer forbear, and in spite of myself my own tears were flowing fast; so that I covered my face and wept over myself; for certainly I was not weeping over him, but at the thought of my own calamity in having lost such a companion. Nor was I the first, for Crito, when he found himself unable to restrain his tears, had got up and moved away, and I followed; and at that moment Apollodorus, who had been weeping all the time, broke out into a loud cry which made cowards of us all. Socrates alone retained his calmness: "What is this strange outcry?" he said. "I sent away the women mainly in order that they might not offend in this way, for I have heard that a man should die in peace. Be quiet, then, and have patience."

When we heard that, we were ashamed, and restrained our tears; and he walked about until, as he said, his legs began to fail, and then he lay on his back, according to the directions, and the man who gave him the poison now and then looked at his feet and legs; and after a while he pressed his foot hard and asked him if he could feel; and he said, "No"; and then his leg, and so upwards and upwards, and showed us that he was cold and stiff. And then Socrates felt them himself, and said, "When the poison reaches the heart, that will be the end." He was beginning to grow cold about the groin, when he uncovered his face (for he had covered himself up) and said— they were his last words—"Crito, I owe a cock to Asclepius; will you remember to pay the debt?" "The debt shall

# 17.  Strengthen Faith to Prevent Fear

WHEN WILL ROGERS was the rage of Broadway, William Fox, the Hollywood mogul, telephoned him one morning at the Ziegfeld Theatre.

"Mr. Rogers," said William Fox, "how would you like to come out to Hollywood and make some pictures for us? We've seen a 'short' you made some time ago. You film well."

Will indicated that he was interested, and an appointment was made. Just before he hung up, William Fox said, "When you come over to keep the appointment you'd better bring your lawyer along to study the contract. We'd like to get going."

Will arrived for the appointment alone. When he was shown into the inner office, he found William Fox flanked by his attorneys. After a brief chat, Fox said, "Where's your lawyer, Will?"

"Aw shucks! I forgot to bring one. How would it be if I dictated a contract? I always fancied I'd like to be a lawyer."

Fox exchanged an amused smile with his attorneys and said, "Okay."

"*Will Rogers agrees to make movies for Fox Films, and*

*Fox Films agrees to pay Will Rogers for making them."*
That's all Will Rogers dictated.

The lawyers of course were horrified at Will's proposal, but Fox agreed to sign it. That was the beginning of a happy and profitable business venture for Rogers and Fox. Together they turned out many films without ever having a disagreement.

Steinmetz, General Electric's great inventor, was also a man of faith. Immersed in his work he didn't want to bother about haggling over a pay check. And so he asked General Electric to keep his bank account large enough to meet his wants. It worked out very well. Neither took advantage of the other because faith prevailed on both sides.

Two of the most admirable brothers I know own an export business in partnership. The older brother started it and brought the younger one to this country later on. They have no formal financial arrangements between them. Each takes what he needs from the business when he needs it. And the business prospers like the green bay tree.

We need so urgently these days to have more faith in people. Within recent years many companies and labor unions have had bitter misunderstandings. Through sharp bargaining and doubts they have sweated and cursed over contracts that too frequently ended in bitterness. For be certain of it, *you can't legislate good faith.*

Some of these contracts approach the ridiculous. Not long ago I read one of fifty-six pages—typed single space on legal-size stationery. The contract specified, among other things, how often you could go to the toilet, what your birthday present from the company was to be, and the like. Despite all the specifications, fear of strikes and retaliations exists all the time on both sides. The root of the trouble of course is simple indeed. There is no faith between them.

How different from the contract recently drawn up with

my friend Frank Dennis in attendance. Frank Dennis is personnel manager of a large chemical company. A new contract with one of the company's unions had to be drawn up.

Frank Dennis chatted informally with the union representatives and said, "How would you like to put your suggestions on the blackboard?" After they did this, he said, "Well, they seem fair enough to me. I believe if I were representing your men, I'd ask for the same things. Now may I list my suggestions alongside yours? If I recommend to top management to sign your suggestions (please notice, he didn't use "demands"), I'd like to include some of my suggestions."

As these were also reasonable suggestions, the union leaders agreed to accept them. There was a fine display of give-and-take. The meeting lasted less than an hour. Everybody went away a winner because good faith prevailed all around the conference table.

Whenever we accept people as real and trustworthy, we display faith. Whenever we adopt an idea as true and obligatory, we display faith. Whenever we look upon the beneficial side of things, we display faith. These attitudes are wholesome. They entail confidence. They make for good human relations. Beyond all else, these attitudes of faith build up feelings of security within those who hold onto them and practice them in their daily contacts.

When we hesitate to put our faith in others we reveal our own self-doubts and unworthiness. We then give a silent testimonial to fear. Common experience as well as statistical studies prove that the vast majority of people are worthy of our faith in them. Did you know that more than 98 per cent of all borrowers repay their indebtedness? Even when their loans are unsecured?

For the sake of our mental health, it is better to bestow our faith in others generally and perhaps run the risk of an occasional disappointment than it is to doubt each individual's trustworthiness until he demonstrates it. Every time we put our faith in others we challenge them to live up to great expectations. Wasn't it Goethe who said, "When you take a man as you find him and do not expect anything too much of him, you leave him poorer than when you found him. But when you take the man and expect great things of him, you leave him nobler than he was before." You also leave yourself nobler.

Modern psychology has pretty conclusively proved that the way we feel toward our fellow man is a reliable index of our attitude toward self. When we expect the worst of others, when we attribute their actions to unworthy motives, we reveal a low opinion of self.

Therefore, the best place to begin to build faith in is ourselves. For my own development cannot get very far until I think well of myself. I must surely love myself—be proud of my values—before I can project a wholesome attitude toward others. And this is a very important part of growth.

In a broad sense, we may say that all people who suffer emotional breakdowns have the feeling of personal unworthiness. Their lack of faith in themselves and in others causes the fear and anxiety that puts them in mental hospitals.

Just think of it: according to Dr. Carney Landis and Dr. J. D. Page, in those American states with the best hospital facilities one person in ten will receive institutional care for mental ailment sometime during his life. These folks experience starvation of faith and love. The reality of their lack is so terrible that they have to escape from it by way of insanity.

Faith in others is synonymous with love. In the First Epistle of St. John (4:7–8) are the words that distill the essence of the Christian faith, "Beloved, let us love one another: for love is of God; and every one that loveth, is born of God, and knoweth God. He that loveth not, knoweth not God; for God is love."

Many are also fearful because they lack faith in God. Blaise Pascal, the great French philosopher, said, "There are only three kinds of persons: those who serve God, having found Him; others who are occupied in seeking Him, not having found Him; while the remainder live without seeking Him, and without having found Him. The first are reasonable and happy, the last are foolish and unhappy; those between are unhappy and reasonable."

Yet I suspect our doubt about the existence of God would take care of itself if we worked harder to establish faith in ourselves and others. We need fewer doubts, more self-assurances. We need to think more about our strengths and purposes; less about our failures and misgivings.

As a civilization I believe we are too intellectual and not intelligent enough. I mean by that, we cultivate the agility of the mind in our educational courses in economics, sociology, physics, and the rest to the neglect of spiritual insight. For example, I have taken more than seventy-five courses in college and university in my time, but I don't recall one professor ever linking his subject matter directly to spiritual values. Good faith was never discussed. For sixteen years I taught in colleges and universities. In all my contacts with colleagues—in faculty meetings, committees, around the lunch table—I don't remember more than one or two specifically relating his field of study to the improvement of the human spirit. They were interested in imparting "objective" information. The pursuit of knowledge for its own end was always their great goal; not as a means of reconciling man to himself, to man, or to God. This is what I mean by our being too intellectual and short on intelligence. Do I make the distinction clear?

'Tis a pity. For our world is more urgently in need of spiritual values than facts and information. We need information but we need it related to the great design. We need right attitudes more than we need doctoral dissertations. Our intellects have the world of substance pretty well under control but the human spirit needs much cultivation. That is why wars, strikes, divorces and other forms of breakdown in human relations constantly threaten to sink us.

Albert Einstein of relativity fame makes the point from a different angle. He says: "What hopes and fears does the scientific method imply for mankind? I do not think that this is the right way to put the question. Whatever this tool in the hand of man will produce depends entirely on the nature of the goals alive in this mankind. Once these goals exist, the scientific method furnishes means to realize them. Yet it cannot furnish the very goals. The scientific method itself would not have led anywhere, it would not even have been born without a passionate striving for clear understanding. Perfection of means and confusion of goals seem—in my opinion —to characterize our age. If we desire sincerely and passionately the safety, the welfare and the free development of the talents of all men, we shall not be in want of the means to approach such a state. Even if only a small part of mankind strives for such goals their superiority will prove itself in the long run."

I often wonder whether we haven't lost many of our goals by giving up some of the old educational practices that emphasized the simple virtues. Take, for example, copybook maxims. Do teachers ever make use of them any more?

Ody H. Lamborn, head of the largest sugar brokerage house in the world, tells the story of his late uncle. Uncle Arthur as a boy attended a Friend's School where he violated some rule. The teacher made him stay after school and write on the blackboard 250 times the saying, "Young men, base all thy actions upon principles of right, always tell the truth, and never fear the consequences."

That experience impressed Uncle Arthur so deeply that his nephew years later could admiringly say, "He ran a fine business. He always told the truth, he was utterly frank, even though he might lose business and money, he never feared the consequences."

What is faith anyway? According to the best educated of the apostles, St. Paul, "Faith is the substance of things hoped for, the evidence of things not seen." It is the heart which experiences faith; not the reason.

Webster gives many definitions, since *faith* has so many uses. But the definition that comes closest to the point I am trying to make is, "The recognition of spiritual realities and moral principles as of paramount authority and supreme value."

When we have faith in Divine Law we have the greatest source of security. We have an answer for all the fears. This business of believing in Divine Law is of course a very personal thing. And one man can do very little to explain it except to recount his own faith in it and perhaps give some examples of how he sees it work.

The largest stock brokerage firm in Wall Street, with more branches throughout the United States than any other brokerage firm, has as its basic business policy: meet the customer's individual investment needs rather than sell him securities. In other words, this business works from a highly ethical premise. What are the results?

One day not long ago a man dressed in a uniform (expect for a felt hat) visited the New York office of this brokerage firm during his lunch hour. He was a doorman at a New York hotel and had saved several hundred dollars which he wanted to invest in common stocks. He wanted a higher return on his money than he was getting, and he wanted the opportunity to see his investment grow.

He was treated with great courtesy and given the cons as well as the pros about investing in common stocks. He was asked to take some literature home to study, literature that outlined an ideal savings program for one in moderate circumstances. Within a day or two he returned and insisted on buying a few shares of a blue-chip common stock.

Some weeks later a woman with a French accent came into the same office to invest almost $2,000.00. She received the same gracious and intelligent service. She was not high-pressured. She was advised to review her insurance and other needs before investing in stocks. But she knew what she wanted. After the transaction, the customer's man said, "May I ask if someone recommended us to you?"

"Yes," she replied, "the doorman of the hotel where I work said that you had been interested in looking out for his welfare. He said that you would give me good advice. So here I am."

Now, many months later an elderly woman came into the same office, leaning on her chauffeur's arm. She wanted help in setting up a half-million dollar trust fund in stocks and bonds for her grandchildren.

And after her business was transacted the customer's man asked her if she would mind telling him who recommended her to his company.

"Oh!" she said. "Marie, my French maid, insisted that I come here. You treated her so kindly and well!"

Evidently the idea of serving each customer's welfare with kindness is right. It brings success. It demonstrates the Divine Law as applied to business.

Here is another example. Many years ago a great man by the name of Charles F. Kettering, of Dayton, Ohio, one morning cranked his automobile. He said, "Certainly there must be a better way of doing this, for I almost broke my arm on this cold morning, trying to crank the darned old car."

That night after work he went out to his little makeshift laboratory and wrote down ten barriers to his discovery of a way to crank an automobile automatically. Then he rearranged those ten steps. He solved the easiest of them first. Then he proceeded to the second step, and so on until he had invented the Delco Self-Starter. He had demonstrated the Law as it applied to mechanics.

Our discovery of the applications of the laws of science has gone on at a breath-taking pace within the last fifty years. The automobile, airplane, tractor-combine, submarine, radio, television, and countless other mechanical things are now our slaves. Yet the physical and mechanical laws that made these machines possible were available to Alexander the Great and Caesar. They were always available.

For man actually creates no natural law. He simply lifts up the curtain from time to time to get another glimpse of the work of the Great Designer. Just as soon as we understand the law that governs the formation of cancer, we shall control it. The law is waiting—it is there—to be discovered.

Today we are turning our attention increasingly to the aspects of the Divine Law that govern human relations and self-understanding. Psychologists suspect that whatever exists, exists in a certain degree or amount and therefore can be measured. And once we can measure, we can control. To be sure, we are still in our swaddling clothes, but we are growing fast. We are searching and seeking and discovering parts of the Divine Law every day. Perhaps fifty years from now our insight into human relations will be as breath-taking as the discovery of the release of fission energy. For Divine Law governs everything. When we obey it and extend our understanding of it, we are happy and successful.

Isn't it significant that the three greatest poems of all the

Western Civilizations—Goethe's *Faust,* Milton's *Paradise Lost,* and Dante's *The Divine Comedy*—all deal with the same underlying thought? *In His will is Man's peace*— These three great poet-philosophers agree that only when we follow Divine Law can we expect first-rate satisfaction from life.

When we use the word "Divine," of course, we run the risk of being misunderstood. For many of us are deeply conditioned by anything that smacks of religion. It's an emotion-charged word. What I have in mind can be found outside the dogmas of the various faiths. One can seek Divine Law and practice it according to his insight without ever going to church. On the other hand, some are so constituted that they need religious services to stimulate them to think about matters of faith and Divine Law.

Dr. Gordon Allport has well said, "Faith is basically man's belief in the validity and attainability of some goal (value)." When we set our goal as faith in mankind, faith in ourselves, and faith in Divine Law, we lead lives free from the devastation of fear.

So long as we commit ourselves to faiths of this sort we need not fear whether we belong to the "right" religious cult. For in the end, each of us must define "religion" and "God" according to his experience and insight.

I personally get a great deal of comfort when I think of this interesting Hindu rite: At about seventeen years of age the Hindu youth receives from his teacher a name for God. This name may be "Beloved" if the youth is unusually affectionate. It may be "Judge" if the youngster's consuming interest is in disputation. It may be "Wisdom" if the youth is contemplative. But each is provided a secret name that fits his temperament, personality, and emotional needs according to his teacher's analysis. This individualized name of God serves to bind the youngster to his Deity. It makes God more approachable, easier to pray to. It encourages the individual to interpret God on a personal plane. It is a source of great comfort to him throughout life.

However we define "God," America is a religious nation. More than 85 per cent of all Americans believe in God. Church attendance is on the increase as is membership in the major faiths. At Northwestern University, Dr. C. S. Braden asked more than two thousand people why they were religious (if they were). There were sixty-five suggested answers in the questionnaire which they filled out. The most commonly endorsed answer was, "Religion gives meaning to life."

Yes, however we define God or religion, or Divine Law, we who believe in *the one increasing purpose of mankind* have something to hold on to. We are not afraid of the epithet hurled at us by the Freudians who say that only those lacking self-sufficiency seek a God. We realize that many have turned to God and religion as a means to solve their fears and worries. (According to one study, 31 per cent of the college students queried said that fear drove them to church.)

For all of us, at times, realize that we need more strength than is found within us. So we turn to a source outside ourselves which we call God or Divine Law or religion. And this source gives us comfort. It encourages us to try again. It gives us, through prayer, an outlet for our tensions. It quickens us to see the miracles about us.

Thoreau said, "To breathe is a miracle!" Isn't it?

Years ago I was connected with a children's clinic where youngsters suffering from cerebral palsy came to learn to walk and talk. The head anatomist there used to say it takes approximately 385 muscles and 222 bones to walk normally; that you can't use them in any way but in the order of a hierarchy. Therefore, every time I see a youngster run down the street I am forced to say, "There goes a miracle!"

The miracle of the galaxies with their infinite space and

the precision with which they adhere to the laws of motion and gravity!— The miracle of the human mind! I walk down Fifth Avenue during the lunch-hour crowds; I see countless faces—but there I recognize the face of a friend! The miracle one experiences with the realization that we can conquer fear by simply changing an attitude! The miracle of speaking into a tiny gadget called a microphone and almost instantaneously being heard around the world!

Yes, as Walt Whitman said, "Why, who speaks to me of miracles"— For he saw miracles everywhere as surely we must.

To sum it up, faith, which is a power that comes with positive thinking, can and does heal us of our wounds. Beyond all else it can, and does, bring us victory over fear!

# Technical Terms for
# Fears and Phobias

ACROPHOBIA. Fear of great heights.
AEROPHOBIA. Fear of heights; drafts.
AGORAPHOBIA. Fear of open places; crowds.
AILUROPHOBIA. Fear of cats.
ALGOPHOBIA. Fear of pain.
ANDROPHOBIA. Fear of man.
ANEMOPHOBIA. Fear of drafts; wind.
ANTHROPHOBIA. Fear of society.
APHEPHOBIA. See HAPHEPHOBIA.
APIPHOBIA. Fear of bees.
ASTRAPHOBIA. Fear of lightning.
ASTROPHOBIA. Fear of solitude; vastness of the heavens.
AUTOPHOBIA. Fear of self or solitude.
BACTERIOPHOBIA. Fear of bacteria.
BASIPHOBIA. Fear of walking.
BASOPHOBIA. Fear of standing upright.
BATHOPHOBIA. Fear of great depths.
BATOPHOBIA. See ACROPHOBIA.
BELONEPHOBIA. Fear of pins; sharp things.
BIBLIOPHOBIA. Dislike of books.
CENOPHOBIA. Fear of large empty rooms.
CHEROPHOBIA. Fear of gaiety.

CLAUSTROPHOBIA. Fear of enclosed spaces.

CLEISIOPHOBIA. See CLAUSTROPHOBIA.

CLEITHROPHOBIA. Fear of being locked in.

CREMNOPHOBIA. Fear of steep places; precipices.

CYNOPHOBIA. Fear of dogs.

CYPRIDOPHOBIA. Fear of syphillis; coitus.

DIPSOPHOBIA. Fear of drink.

DYSMORPHOPHOBIA. Fear of deformity.

EREMOPHOBIA. See AGORAPHOBIA.

EREMIOPHOBIA. Fear of stillness.

EREUTHOPHOBIA. Fear of blushing.

ERGASIOPHOBIA. Fear of surgical operations; of work. See PONOPHOBIA.

EROTOPHOBIA. Dislike of sexual talk.

ERYTHROPHOBIA. Fear of red.

GALEOPHOBIA. *See* AILUROPHOBIA.

GAMOPHOBIA. Fear of marriage.

GATOPHOBIA. *See* AILUROPHOBIA.

GEPHYROPHOBIA. Fear of crossing a bridge.

GYMNOPHOBIA. Fear of nakedness.

GYNECOPHOBIA. Fear of women.

HAPHEPHOBIA. Fear of being touched.

HYDROPHOBIA. Fear of water; symptoms of rabies. See LYSSO-PHOBIA.

HYGROPHOBIA. Fear of dampness.

ICHTHYOPHOBIA. Fear of fish.

KERAUNOPHOBIA. Fear of lightning.

KLEPTOPHOBIA. Fear of becoming a thief.

LALOPHOBIA. Fear of speech.

LYSSOPHOBIA. Fear of rabies. See HYDROPHOBIA.

MAIEUSIOPHOBIA. Fear of childbirth.

MERINTHOPHOBIA. Fear of being bound.

MYSOPHOBIA. Fear of dirt.

MYTHOPHOBIA. Fear of lies.

NECROPHOBIA. Fear of death.

NEOPHOBIA. Fear of new scenes.

NYCTOPHOBIA. Fear of darkness.

OCHLOPHOBIA. Fear of crowds. See AGOROPHOBIA.

ODYNOPHOBIA. Fear of pain. See ALGOPHOBIA.

OPHIDIOPHOBIA. See OPHIOPHOBIA.

OPHIOPHOBIA. Fear of snakes.

OSMOPHOBIA. Fear of smells.

PANOPHOBIA. Fear of everything.

PHARMACOPHOBIA. Fear of drugs.

PHENOPHOBIA. Fear of light.

PHOBOPHOBIA. Fear of being afraid or alarmed.

PHONOPHOBIA. Fear of sound or noise.

PHOTOPHOBIA. See PHENOPHOBIA.

PHRONEMOPHOBIA. Fear of thinking.

PNIGOPHOBIA. Fear of choking, as in angina pectoris.

PONOPHOBIA. Fear of work.

PSYCHROPHOBIA. Fear of cold.

PYROPHOBIA. Fear of fire.

RHYPOPHOBIA. Fear of filth.

RUPOPHOBIA. Dislike of dirt.

SCOPOPHOBIA. Fear of being stared at.

SIDEROPHOBIA. Fear of railroad travelling.

SITIOPHOBIA. Fear of food.

SITOPHOBIA. See SITIOPHOBIA.

TAPHOPHOBIA. Fear of being buried alive.

TERATOPHOBIA. Fear of deformed persons; of giving birth to
     a teras.

THALASSOPHOBIA. Fear of the sea.

THANATOPHOBIA. Fear of death.

TOXICOPHOBIA. Fear of poison.

TOXIPHOBIA. See TOXICOPHOBIA.

XENOPHOBIA. Fear of meeting strangers.

ZOOPHOBIA. Fear of animals.

# Bibliography

Allport, Gordon W., *The Individual and His Religion*. New York: The Macmillan Co.

Beers, Clifford, *The Mind That Found Itself*. Garden City: Doubleday & Co., Inc.

Branden, C. S., "Why People Are Religious"—a study in religious motivation. *The Journal of Bible and Religion*, 1947, 15, 38-45.

Bullis, H. Edmund & O'Malley, Emily E., *Human Relations in the Classroom*. Wilmington, Del.: Delaware State Society for Mental Hygiene.

Cannon, Walter B., *Bodily Changes in Fear, Hunger, Pain and Rage*. New York: Appleton-Century-Crofts, Inc.

Clark, Le Mon, *Sex and You*. Indianapolis: The Bobbs-Merrill Company.

Coué, Émile, *Autosuggestion*. New York: The McBride Company, Inc.

Crile, George W., *Man: An Adaptive Mechanism*. New York: Appleton-Century-Crofts, Inc.

Dubois, Paul, *Self-Control and How to Secure It*. New York: Funk & Wagnalls.

Einstein, Albert, *Out of My Later Years*. New York: Philosophical Library.

Fisher, James T. and Hawlett, Lowell S., *A Few Buttons Missing: The Case of a Psychiatrist*. Philadelphia: J. B. Lippincott Co.

Flammarion, Camille, *Death and Its Mystery*. New York: Appleton-Century-Crofts, Inc.

Gumpert, Martin, *You Are Younger Than You Think*. New York: Duell, Sloane & Pearce.

Harwood, E. C. & Fowler, Helen, *How to Make Your Budget Balance*. Cambridge, Mass.: Am. Inst. for Economic Research.

James, William, *Varieties of Religious Experience*. New York: Henry Holt & Co.

Jersild, Arthur, *Children's Fears*. New York: Teachers College, Bureau of Publications, Columbia University.

Kitson, Harry D., *How to Use Your Mind*. Philadelphia: J. B. Lippincott Co.

Landis, Carney & Page, J. D., *Modern Society & Mental Disease*. New York: Farrar & Rinehart.

Magoun, F. Alexander, *Love and Marriage*. New York: Harper & Brothers.

May, Rollo, *Problem of Anxiety*. New York: Ronald Press.

McCarthy, Mary, *Handicaps*. London: Longman's, Green & Co., Inc.

Munro, D. G. Macleod, *The Psychopathology of Tuberculosis*. London: Oxford University Press.

Murchison, Carl, *Handbook of Child Psychology*, 2nd ed. Worcester, Mass.: Clark University Press.

Peale, Norman Vincent & Blanton, Smiley, *The Art of Real Happiness*. New York: Prentice-Hall, Inc.

The *Performance* of Physically Impaired Workers in Manufacturing Industries. Bulletin No. 923 United States Department of Labor Statistics, 1948, 132 pages.

Read, Grantly, *Childbirth Without Pain*. New York: Paul B. Hoeber, Inc.

Rhoades, Winfred, *The Self You Have to Live With*. Philadelphia: J. B. Lippincott Co.

Saperstein, M. R., *Emotional Security*. New York: Crown Publishers.

Sheehan, Vincent, *Not Peace But a Sword*. Garden City: Doubleday & Co., Inc.

Smith, G. Milton, *More Power to Your Mind*. New York: Harper & Brothers.

Spock, Benjamin, *Baby and Child Care*. New York: Pocket Books, Inc.

Stokes, Walter R., *Modern Pattern for Marriage*. New York: Rinehart & Co.

Weber, F. Parkes, *Aspects of Death & Correlated Aspects of Life*. London: T. F. Unwin, Ltd.

Weiss, Edward and English, O. Spurgeon, *Psychosomatic Medicine*. Baltimore: W. B. Saunders Co.

Wylie, Berdett (ed.), *Sex and Marriage: A Guide to Marital Relations*. Cleveland: World Publishing Co.

# Index